SLAYING BOSTON

Curated by Leigh M. Clark

Aurora Corialis Publishing

Pittsburgh, PA

Printed in the United States of America
Edited by: Renee Picard, Aurora Corialis Publishing
Cover Design: Leigh M. Clark
Paperback ISBN: 978-1-958481-50-9
Ebook ISBN: 978-1-958481-51-6

OTHER COLLECTIVES BY LEIGH M. CLARK

Slaying Southwest Florida

Slaying Tampa Bay

Slaying Atlanta

Slaying Nashville

Slaying Sarasota

Slaying Chicago

Slaying Las Vegas

The Dream is in Your Hands

The Dream is in Your Hands: She Can Do It

Living Kindly: Bold Conversations About the Power of

Kindness

Table of Contents

Introduction: Slaying Boston – A City of Strength and Story

Leigh M. Clark

The first time I visited Boston, I was in my twenties. My brother had just graduated college and was living in a small apartment near Fenway. It was a quick visit, just a few days, but something about the city stayed with me. A few years later, I returned for a job interview and spent more time walking the grounds of Cambridge, exploring Harvard, and getting a stronger sense of what Boston stood for. Even though I've never lived here, Boston has always held a quiet place in my memory—a place where history and ambition feel tightly woven together.

Today, my brother and his family live in Longmeadow, and it's been beautiful to watch their roots grow in Massachusetts. While it's not quite the city, there's something about having family nearby that makes this project feel personal. Getting to share the stories of women who are shaping Boston's present and future is both a privilege and a responsibility I don't take lightly.

Slaying Boston is the seventh book in the Slay the USA series, and if there's one thing we know about this city, it's that it doesn't sit still. Boston is constantly evolving. It's a city built on legacy but driven by innovation. From higher education and healthcare to journalism, biotech, the arts, and social entrepreneurship, Boston is a hub of big ideas—and women are at the forefront of nearly every sector.

This book isn't just about highlighting professional success. It's about honoring women who have found the courage to live their truth. Women who are building, leading, advocating, creating, healing, and lifting others along the way. The women in this book are Emmy-winning journalists, celebrated artists, founders of thriving startups, nonprofit leaders, educators, doctors, and rising voices across countless industries. Some are nationally recognized. Others are just beginning to make waves. But every single one of them has something meaningful to say— and their stories have the power to inspire.

In Boston, that energy is everywhere. Women here are innovating in tech labs, treating patients in world-class hospitals, teaching in classrooms, and bringing visibility to underrepresented communities. They're shaping policy at the local level, breaking new ground in media, and using creativity to drive social change.

According to recent reports, Massachusetts ranks among the top states for women in leadership, education, and healthcare access. Women make up nearly fifty percent of the state's labor force, and in the Greater Boston area, the number of women-owned businesses continues to grow steadily each year. In industries like biotech, higher education, and financial services, Boston remains one of the most competitive metro areas in the country—yet it's also increasingly becoming one of the most collaborative, with women leading cross-sector innovation, mentorship networks, and support systems designed to ensure no one has to build alone.

We're seeing a significant shift in the city's leadership, too. Boston elected its first woman and first person of color as mayor in 2021, and today, the city council includes a majority of women. These aren't just milestones. They're signals that the narrative is expanding—making space for more voices, more stories, and more representation.

But Slaying Boston goes deeper than a highlight reel. At its core, this project is about authenticity. To slay doesn't mean to be perfect—it means to leave your mark. It's about showing up fully, embracing your story, and knowing that your impact matters. Every woman featured in this book has done that in her own way. Some through resilience. Some through reinvention. All through a sense of purpose.

Boston is known for being one of the most educated cities in the country, home to more than 50 colleges and universities. But beyond the degrees and accolades, there's a culture of intention here. People come to Boston to build, to explore, and to push limits—and that's exactly what the women in this book are doing. They're not here to play small. They're here to shape lives, institutions, and communities.

You'll meet women who have created safe spaces, launched life-changing businesses, stood up for what's right, and reinvented themselves after personal upheaval. These are not stories polished for perfection—they're shared to offer connection. Because when one woman shares her truth, it gives another woman permission to speak hers.

What I love most about curating these books is that every chapter feels like a thread in a larger tapestry. No two journeys are the same, but there's a shared rhythm: a desire to rise, to impact, to live with purpose. And Boston, with all its grit, intelligence, history, and drive, is the perfect setting for that kind of narrative.

Slaying Boston is a tribute—not just to achievement, but to authenticity. To women who are stepping forward in their lives, not because the path was easy, but because it mattered. To women who aren't afraid to ask better questions, build new tables, and reimagine what's possible.

I'm proud to share this collection with you. I hope it makes you feel seen, empowered, and connected. Most of all, I hope it reminds you that no matter where you are or what chapter you're in—your voice, your truth, and your impact matter.

Boston, thank you for the women you've raised, supported, and inspired. This book is for you.

To "SLAY" or Be Slayed...

Jackie Bruno

For a long time, I thought these were my two options: to succeed or to fail. That you either did one or the other.

When I was asked to write this first chapter of a book about women slaying in my hometown of Boston, I thought, *absolutely*! *What a great opportunity!* But when the time came to put pen to paper—or really, words into Word—I felt more exhausted than elated. I almost tried to back out!

This may come as a surprise because if you look at my Instagram page, it definitely looks like I'm slaying—and it should. That's my personal PR page, and I'm pretty good at PR! I own and operate a public relations company called Newsmaker Marketing. My job is to make our clients look good, and we do. Newsmaker Marketing is one of Boston's fastest-growing PR companies.

I'm also a former journalist who left a fifteen-year career in TV news because I had simply burned out. Sounds bad—but I even found a way to flip that story into a "slay" moment: I wrote an article for *Boston Magazine* explaining why I burned out, and how that gave me the clarity to start my company. Surprisingly, being honest about hard times can be inspiring to others. But here's the problem: it's only considered inspiring if it has a happy ending.

That article did have a happy ending—or so I thought. I had found a way past burnout and toward professional success. Slay! But the story didn't end there. The time that followed was the opposite of happy. Working from home made me realize my marriage was deeply flawed—beyond repair. I was faced with an incredibly difficult decision: leave and break up my family, or stay and sacrifice myself.

I chose me.

I chose the me I *could* be, and I'm working my way to her now.

Over the past few years, I've left my chosen career, my husband, and the home we bought together. I've had to look into the faces of my babies and break their hearts, giving them news that I knew would absolutely crush them. I've had to rebuild my relationship with them and earn back their trust.

This decision hasn't just crushed others—it's crushed me too. Every other Monday, I send my boys off to school knowing that for the next week, I'll be on the outside of their lives. I can check in with calls and maybe a quick visit, but for that next week, they're on the other side of the divide—a divide I chose.

In many ways, my definition of "slay" has evolved into something closer to survival. I'm no longer just proud of the moments you see on Instagram. I'm most proud of the moments you don't see. The moments I got out of bed when I just wanted to hide under the covers. The moments I put on a happy face so my boys could feel joy, even when I didn't. The moments I admitted defeat and asked for help.

I'm here to tell you that slaying isn't a solo sport. Sometimes, you need an army—or better yet, a small but mighty militia.

When I left my home after my marriage ended, my parents were my saviors. They didn't judge. They let me slink back to my childhood bedroom—not exactly where you expect to be at the end of your thirties—and found ways to normalize an incredibly abnormal time for me and my boys. After a few months, they helped me get my own townhouse, and I began the process of making it my new home.

My mother, bless her heart, is quite the authority on home décor. She has great taste and can be critical when others' choices differ from her own. However, in this new space, she bit her tongue and turned a blind eye, letting me do what I wanted— even though she technically owned the place (I rent it).

I was meticulous about picking out the furniture and décor, proud to buy them myself and downright giddy that the only person they had to please was me! Most of the home is an elegant blend of neutral colors, with one exception: I made my bedroom an ode to my favorite muses—Dolly Parton and Jackie O! There's even a Wonder Woman painting to remind me that women are superheroes.

When it came time to reveal my masterpiece, my mom admitted it kind of worked and joked, "No man would ever want to enter a room so girly!"

I've since tested that theory—and I can report that they are still eager to get the chance!

Yet, despite this discovery, I'm not exactly slaying this area of my life. I've found that when it comes to available (or seemingly available) men, there are more frogs than princes. Let's face it—finding a desirable man after divorce is like finding a designer bag in a clearance bin. Nearly impossible. And even if you do find one, you can't help but wonder, *How in the hell did this end up here?!* (Note: They're usually damaged.)

I can laugh about most of it now, but there were times I was truly devastated—shocked by betrayal, questioning whether I'd die alone. Thankfully, my two best friends never let me feel truly alone.

Andrea and Nicole called every week to check in. They knew I needed them, and they took that responsibility seriously. Most of the time, we'd laugh as I recounted my bumbling attempts at dating. But in my lowest moments, they showed me the true meaning of friendship—offering love and patience during a time when I had little left to give in return.

Through all of this, I somehow built a successful business—but I'd be lying if I said I did it alone. Newsmaker Marketing would have put me in the grave if I didn't have my incredible partners, Rachel Robbins and Liam Martin, and our first employee, Michaela Forbes. They kept the company running, even when I couldn't, and they gave me the grace to grieve without judgment.

I definitely slayed when I picked this team.

Together, we've lifted each other up, filled in the blanks when another couldn't, and poured all that collective love back into our clients.

These experiences have taught me that you can, in fact, slay while feeling slayed. It's not either-or. Not black or white. Life is a messy mix of ups and downs, and sometimes, we have to call in the reserves.

As you read the next chapters from some of Boston's most accomplished women, I hope you put less emphasis on the outcome or the need for a happy ending. Instead, I hope you see that the real glory is in the battle—because without adversity, we'd have nothing to slay!

About the Author

You may recognize Jackie Bruno from the news. She spent ten years anchoring and reporting at NECN and NBC 10 Boston. Before that, she was a trusted source in Springfield, Mass., where she worked as an anchor and reporter.

Now, Jackie is the proud owner, founder, and CEO of Newsmaker Marketing, a public relations firm that is revolutionizing PR for the digital age. Her team of former journalists can not only get press for your company thanks to their deep relationships, but they can also tell your story directly using video production, expert storytelling, and social media content creation. Newsmaker Marketing represents a growing list of clients including Cyclyx, LexRx, Babson Alumni, and Shields Health.

Additionally, Jackie is an ardent supporter of women. She is a member of the alumni mentorship program at Boston University, where she graduated with honors in 2006. She also is the founder of The Connect-Her: a networking organization to help professional women achieve their personal and professional goals. Jackie believes that female friendship and support are critical for women throughout their lives. It's a lesson she first learned in pageants, after representing Massachusetts nationally at two: Miss Teen USA where she made the top five and Miss USA where she placed in the top ten.

Jackie is also the mom of two boys Jack and James, and her beloved Shih Tzu buddy.

https://newsmakermarketing.com

Instagram: @TheJackieBruno and @NewsmakerMarketing

Never Give Up, and the Power of Endless Possibilities

Angela Aslami

On November 26, 1932, my maternal great-grandfather's corpse was tossed onto our family courtyard in Afghanistan. He had been the Afghan deputy foreign minister in Paris and Moscow. Chaos ensued. The women and children were rounded up and thrown in prison, including my maternal grandfather, who was then age six, and maternal grandmother, then age 11. The adult men were imprisoned and subsequently executed, and the teenage boys were separately imprisoned. The events leading up to this included the 1929 overthrow of the king (whom my great-grandparents served). This was followed by the new king's family friends and soldiers "loyal" to him consolidating power and ultimately destroying the former king's officers, including my family. In response to these atrocities, our family servant assassinated the new king, whose brother assumed power and took no mercy on our family. They were released from prison 14 years later and remained under house arrest for five more years. Many perished in prison from infections, starvation, and abuse. This early Afghan history is detailed in two books, *From My Memories* published by my grandfather in 2010, and *Shackled*, published by my cousin in 2017.

Both of my parents were born and raised in Afghanistan. They came to the United States in the 1960s to study, with no intention of settling here permanently. My father completed his Ph.D. in 1971, the same year I was born, and worked here until 1977, at which time he took a teaching assignment at a Saudi Arabian university. I attended first and second grade in Saudi Arabia. We lived in a gated community with other westerners, segregated from Saudi society so as not to "corrupt" them. My mom wasn't allowed to drive or work or go anywhere without my father. She was the most spectacular woman on earth, in my eyes, and I resented how the Saudis treated her. The Soviet Union's 1979 Afghanistan invasion kicked off never-ending wars that permanently derailed my family's return to their homeland.

My mother was the oldest of four, and my father was the second oldest of ten. She was a homemaker and worked tirelessly to bring their families out of Soviet-occupied Afghanistan. I was often sad that my parents weren't on the sidelines cheering at my soccer games, but now, I realize how urgent and frantic their survival guilt must have been after my father's brother was killed by the Soviets in a demonstration against occupation.

All twelve of my aunts and uncles came to live with us in Massachusetts at one point or another on their journey to rebuild their lives, and they have since settled in the United States and Germany. They married Afghans and created traditional families.

I am the second oldest of the twenty-eight kids in my generation, eighteen of whom are women. Fifteen of these women blossomed into two doctors, two lawyers, an accountant, a pharmaceutical executive, a Cal-Fire researcher, a hotel and restaurant start-up consultant, an engineer, a biomedical researcher, an international fashion designer, a fashion consultant, a school secretary, a college-endowment fund developer, and a stay-at-home mom with five children. The remaining three young women are currently in college studying nursing or business. We were encouraged (and expected) to go to college and pursue careers. My mother and aunts told us often, "You need to take advantage of the opportunities we didn't have." My family has truly embodied the American (and European) dream, demonstrating the power and wisdom of women free from Soviet and Taliban oppression. These women have saved lives (medically, legally and economically), created jobs, cured genetic diseases, educated countless students, and prevented millions of acres of forest land and homes from burning. These are my sisters and first cousins, and their world impact is due to the tenacity of their immigrant parents.

My early career plan was to become a judge in family court working against domestic violence after witnessing an incident in my extended family. I was accepted into law school after graduating from American University in Washington, D.C., with a major in political science and a minor in women's studies. A shoulder surgery before graduation necessitated spending a lot of time in physical therapy, and I really appreciated the personal care I received. I had always been a bit of a "health nut," focusing on sunscreen, helmets, vitamins, and nutrition since middle school, and the intense exposure to the medical field during my shoulder recovery ultimately propelled me to drop the idea of going to law school. Instead, I became a doctor, believing that I could have a more lasting impact on people with the long-term relationships formed inside doctor-patient relationships.

Pursuing a career in obstetrics and gynecology was a natural extension of my interest in improving the lives of women and children. I married in 1998 and had five children, including two sets of twins through fertility treatments. Sadly, that marriage ended recently. I wanted, expected, and believed in the ability to "work hard and have it all," "all" being defined as family, career and economic independence. I've since learned how badly even United States career women struggle with economic independence due to patriarchal norms, inherent bias against women, and the lack of equal rights and equal pay, even among doctors. For example, female-dominated specialties such as obstetrics and gynecology earn forty percent less than male-dominated specialties like orthopedic surgery despite the same time commitments for education and training and owing to government and insurance fee schedules created by (and for the benefit of) male breadwinners. Working mothers, myself included, frequently reduce career time for pregnancies, breastfeeding, and mothering, resulting in a flattening of earning potential compared to fathers. When marriages fall apart, the male-dominated family court system is left to equalize family economics, and this has been an abysmal failure across the country.

Experiencing a multicultural upbringing, marriage, fertility problems, parenting, divorce, and the heartbreak of caring for my mom through a terminal illness has enabled me to deeply relate with the struggles many women have. Adding board certifications in obesity medicine and functional medicine has allowed me to expand my patient care approach. Early in my career, a patient's complaint of constipation and bloating would result in a stool softener recommendation. Now, those symptoms become a long conversation about exactly what, when, and how the patient eats, how the gut works, the importance of micronutrients (magnesium, for example), and the interplay between stress, sleep, and hormones. My recommendations now are much more comprehensive. Some of my patients even send their husbands, who now proudly tell their guy friends that their "gynecologist is my favorite doctor," and we all have a good laugh. While I absolutely believe in this comprehensive care model, it is completely incompatible with the traditional corporate business model where patients are scheduled every fifteen minutes.

In 2015, a dear friend and colleague asked if I wanted to move my practice from the hospital to his newly constructed medical building. I jumped at the chance; however, the main problem was that "my practice" wasn't "my practice," as I was a hospital employee. Nevertheless, I trusted him completely. We are kindred spirits who have been attending the same church for years, and we both juggle busy medical practices with raising large families.

I opened Horizons Health and Wellness in 2016, a vision based on my 1994 medical school entrance exam essay and now my dream come true. As any small business owner will tell you, sometimes it's a nightmare. At the time, my five children were ages four through ten, and creating my own practice gave me the flexibility to get home earlier, give up hospital nights, weekends, and holidays, be more present for my kids, and deliver care on my terms. We have no double-booked appointments, no appointments less than thirty minutes, with complementary offerings for nutrition, weight management, hormone therapy, and aesthetics. We offer resources to help women navigate the complexities of being a woman, including parenting, marriage, divorce, caring for aging parents, self-care, and balancing careers with family responsibilities. We provide a safe space for women to talk about everything affecting their lives and health. An appointment in our office is a cross between therapy, pap smears, beauty treatments, and future planning.

I have had the privilege of delivering babies, caring for them as teenagers, shepherding their mothers through menopause and their grandmothers through surgeries, and even attending a few funerals. Patients from South and Central America, Africa, Europe, Australia, China, India, and the rest of Asia have taught me that family themes are universal no matter the heritage: mothers are the family backbone and the cultural anchor through recipes, music, dances, family gatherings, and holiday traditions passed down from one generation to the next.

I know my great grandparents would be so proud knowing that their children escaped political prisons and created an enduring legacy of survivors who have provided opportunities, created jobs, saved lives, prevented environmental catastrophes and started multiple businesses across three continents. I'm so proud to be part of this exceptional family. The personal is indeed political. I live by what the great Winston Churchill said: "Never, ever, ever give up."

About the Author

Dr. Angela Aslami is a board-certified OB/GYN, obesity medicine specialist and functional medicine/sexual health practitioner based in the Boston area, with over twenty-five years of experience. She earned her medical degree from Wake Forest University and completed her residency at Carolinas Medical Center. She has practiced at Greenwich Hospital in Connecticut, as well as Good Samaritan Medical Center, Brockton Hospital and Milton Hospital (all three in Massachusetts). In 2016, she founded Horizons Health and Wellness in Bridgewater, Mass., an independent medical practice delivering comprehensive care in a relaxed environment.

Passionate about a holistic approach to healthcare, Dr. Aslami integrates nutritional and functional medicine with traditional gynecological care. She provides expert menopause and perimenopause management and helps women of all ages live, look, and feel their best throughout their lifespan by incorporating aesthetic services, micronutrient support and guidance, weight management, fitness guidance, emotional support, hormone therapy, and sexual health services. Her desire is to provide comprehensive care tailored to each woman.

A daughter of Afghan immigrants, Dr. Aslami has studied and traveled across the globe. She has developed a broad perspective on healthcare, blending science with a personalized approach. She believes in empowering women through education and proactive wellness strategies.

Dr. Aslami lives in the Boston area with her five children, balancing her thriving career with an active family life. When she's not in the office, she enjoys biking, hiking, skiing, traveling, and attending church services.

www.horizonshealthandwellness.com

Let Your Rebel Soul Bloom

Rebecca Borges

As I stood in the small kitchen of my Beacon Hill apartment on Myrtle Street staring at the letter in my hand from Massachusetts College of Art, I felt a flurry of emotions rising within me. My astonishment and loss for words was quickly followed by a flash of anger and an outburst of "FUCK WHAT THEY THINK!" before crumpling the letter and throwing it to the floor. My pup, who'd been sitting cheerfully in front of me, waiting for her evening walk, put her ears back and quizzically cocked her head sensing my anger, and likely hoping it wasn't directed toward her.

My roommate, who was in med school at the time, cautiously called out from the other room, "Hey, is something... wrong?"

"It looks like I just got expelled from art school," I responded.

He laughed, "Who the hell gets expelled from art school?"

Well... as it turns out, apparently I do.

———

It was the end of my second year at Massachusetts College of Art (MassArt) in their fashion design program—and I was in deep shit. The faculty felt I had been disparaging to the efforts of my peers and the fashion design industry in general. My final project, which I affectionately refer to as my *pièce de resistance*, a semi-transparent wedding gown featuring a twenty-foot train that acted as a noose with a hem that hobbled the model's runway walk, was a step too far for all the jurors. In fact, my garment caused such a ruckus during our runway presentation that the school's dean of architecture, also one of the jurors, called for a halt to the show and a pause to the feedback in order to end the incredibly loud criticism and berating I was receiving from at least two indignant jurors.

Perhaps I should not have been surprised by the disciplinary letter given the extremely negative feedback I received during the final presentation. However, technically, my garments were correct. I had been sewing since I was a young girl, taught by my mother, who learned as part of her home economics classes taken while she was in high school. I knew how to sew better than most of my classmates and even some of the faculty members of the fashion design department. I even finished several garments with a French seam, a technical seam which my instructor was unfamiliar with, but I digress.

In the end, my work had struck a nerve. To the department, my use of sandpaper, salvaged and commercial materials, metals, wire, and transparent fabrics wasn't creative; it was crude. And they'd seen my preference towards utilitarian and commercial-grade materials as offensive, not explorative.

It also turns out that my passion for creating garments addressing the historical exploitation of women and social constructs was just a step too far for MassArt's fashion department. I mean... I knew I was pushing the envelope when I made a dress from sandpaper. Hell, my fingers were literally bleeding while creating that one. But my *pièce de resistance*, the wedding gown, was a step too far. The disciplinary letter I received that fateful day in my Beacon Hill kitchen clearly stated that I'd strayed down a path that would not be tolerated. Apparently, conformity, to the fashion design department parameters, to societal ideals of fashion, and the constructs of acceptable beauty, were necessary for me to continue my education at MassArt.

In the grand scheme of things, being expelled wasn't my only problem. I'd been halfway through my program and at the end of my second year when the disciplinary letter arrived—which wasn't ideal. I had spent three years applying for acceptance to MassArt all while working full-time and taking art classes at The University of Massachusetts in Boston to build my portfolio. There was also the financial factor. MassArt was the only state-funded art school in the country, which had made my tuition bill, footed solely by me, manageable. In thinking about the five years and thousands of dollars I had invested in this pursuit, it was difficult to not wonder if it had all been in vain.

Unbeknownst to me at the time, my path as a sculptor had begun while at MassArt. I explored Boston in search of random materials for use in my designs, rummaging through small, long-standing neighborhood hardware stores, metal scrap yards, and dumpsters in the leather district. My curiosity to explore new materials had become the prelude to 3D work that would eventually find the limitations of the human shape a bore, in part because I had been sewing for over a decade already. Still, I couldn't wrap my head around attending art school and conforming at the same time. These were simply two scenarios that felt in complete juxtaposition to me.

Even as I think about the situation today, thirty years later, I still find myself shaking my head at the irony of it all. Looking back, it's hard to remember exactly how long I spent wallowing after receiving the letter. Thankfully, my negative feelings were replaced by a need to move forward and continue creating. I was encouraged to move forward by a supportive mother, a few instructors from MassArt, and one very good friend who thrived on being a contrarian.

Eventually, sometime that summer, the little rebel sitting inside my soul prodded me... I mean really, *who the fuck were they to say my work was shit*?

Instead of giving up, I applied to five other art schools across the country. With acceptance to four of the five, I left Boston in 1994 to finish my art education in the Windy City at the prestigious School of the Art Institute in Chicago (SAIC). I may have been expelled from MassArt, but my artistic spirit remained unbroken. And having my portfolio accepted at four top-tier art schools was just what my rebel soul needed to continue. What I didn't know at the time, couldn't possibly know at the time, was this rebellious act would be the catalyst for a journey that would redefine my life.

Please don't let me mislead you. My start in Chicago was a far cry from sunshine and roses. *Fuck what they think* became my silent mantra as I forged on during my first year in SAIC's fashion department amidst challenges similar to those I experienced at MassArt. There was one key difference: SAIC's department advisors were invested in me and determined to find an approach to my continued creative development. In fact, it was SAIC's multidisciplinary approach that nurtured my creative spirit. My faculty advisors found, and encouraged me to attend, a furniture design program in England offered during the summer between my third and fourth years. By the time I returned to SAIC in the fall of 1995, a whole new world had opened for me.

In resisting MassArt's attempt to make me conform I eventually learned that the only limitations I truly have are the ones I place on myself, something I've needed to remind myself of many times over. Leaving MassArt, Boston, and my entire family pushed me to explore, find my voice as an artist, and bloom in a garden where I had a say in what would grow around me. I flourished as an artist for many years in Chicago, enjoying participation in summer art fairs and gallery shows. My work was unique and unlike anything I had seen before and I loved sharing it with others. And though my work was not a huge financial success, the joy it brought me was enough. Until it wasn't.

Like most artists, I had another job—two in fact. "Daylighting" in a law firm paid my bills and rent while "moonlighting" as a bartender paid my student loans. And yes, I needed both. Fearful that my unique sculpture would never truly be lucrative, I refused to become a "starving artist" and created a world for myself which prevented that from happening. Unfortunately, it also left me little time to actually create.

Determined to forge my own path, I struggled with the inequity of time for years while attempting to find some kind of balance between making money and creating one-of-a-kind furniture and sculpture before finally deciding to obtain a master's in landscape architecture. As my work evolved to include a handful of exterior metal sculptures and architectural details for luxury residential homes in Chicago, landscape architecture felt harmonic to my continued creative growth. Why not literally plant the garden around my sculptural creations?

Borges Design, founded upon graduation from The School of the Art Institute of Chicago, continues to be the umbrella under which I practice as a sculptor and landscape designer. My latest endeavor, Plant Happy, seeks to help people revive their connection to the natural world by inviting plants, real, preserved, and faux, into the spaces where we live, work and play to increase creativity, promote overall well-being, and reduce stress.

My path has been far from linear. I have faced rejection, expulsion, employment terminations, and many failures along the way. With each of these turning points there have been opportunities to redefine my art and to push my creative boundaries to create something that moves me, and hopefully others, emotionally. In returning to Boston I feel I have come full circle. The student once deemed too unorthodox has reshaped herself and ground around her.

It was nearly twenty-six years to the day when I returned to Boston with many *fuck what they think* muttered under my breath. I reconnected with MassArt, the scene of the crime, to view an alumni show, which presented me with an opportunity to reflect on my journey. In returning, I have had time to contemplate why I left in the first place and acknowledge that being expelled from art school is an important part of my story. More importantly, it has not been a part of my story I previously embraced as it was too damn easy to gloss over. Until I returned to Boston I had not understood that glossing over this part of my story didn't allow me the benefit of seeing it for what it truly was: a unique opportunity. An opportunity to remember my strengths, the value of failure, and how being rebellious can be really, really good for your soul.

About the Author

Rebecca Borges is a born and raised New Englander who returned to her roots after a twenty-six-year detour to the Midwest by way of Chicago. Led by her rebel soul to leave Boston and pursue fashion design, Rebecca attended the prestigious School of the Art Institute of Chicago, obtaining a BFA rooted in fashion, sculpture, and architecture. It was this multi-disciplinary education that gave birth to Borges Design.

Over the years Rebecca has worked in many mediums and with various materials, including fabric, non-traditional textiles, wood, steel, copper, and glass. Through the various iterations and explorations of material and medium, nature has been her muse. So, at forty years young, with dozens of summer art festivals under her belt selling and exhibiting her one-of-a-kind sculptural furniture and architectural details, she turned her full attention to nature and successfully obtained her master's degree in landscape architecture.

Because employment prospects were dreary and entry-level salaries were at an all-time low for newly graduated landscape architects, Rebecca took another detour. This time it was all about finding her tribe, which ultimately brought her to FemCity where she led the Chicago community for six years.

During the 2021 global pandemic, FemCity Chicago floundered, and countless individuals were confined to their homes. So Rebecca launched Plant Happy, a biophilic design studio that wholeheartedly embraces the mission to rekindle mankind's bond with nature. Using her multifaceted expertise as a metal sculptor, artist, and landscape architect.

Today, Rebecca employs the transformative power of art and design to infuse the spaces where we work, live and play with the rejuvenating essence of the natural world. After spending nearly thirty years in Chicago, Rebecca recognizes the pressing significance of reconnecting with nature, especially in big cities, and passionately champions the cause knowing many individuals lack easy access to the beauty of the natural world.

Ever inspired by the captivating allure of Mother Nature, Rebecca skillfully works plants into her creations, much like a painter deftly wields their brush. To her, "painting with plants" is an embodiment of an enchanting ambiance. Imagine a home devoid of conventional artwork, yet brimming with lush foliage— from this plant-filled sanctuary comes an irresistible warmth, inviting tranquility and vibrant energy.

Rebecca believes that everyone deserves to live and work in spaces that inspire true emotional connection, and makes it her mission to help people connect with Mother Nature through art and design.

Beyond her unique work as a sculptor, Rebecca uses real and preserved plant materials to create living walls and gorgeous garden designs. She is passionate about the awe-inspiring beauty of nature, and strives to bring visions of lush, plant-filled spaces to life. With Rebecca's dedication, artistry, and expertise, she'll take you on a transformative journey that reunites you with the natural world, fostering a profound connection that transcends the boundaries of mere aesthetics.

Rebecca's passion for the natural world has been featured in the *Chicago Tribune*, *Absolute Artistry* on PBS, and WGN Chicago with *Market Overdrive*.

www.BorgesDesign.com
www.PlantHappy.com
https://www.facebook.com/Rebecca.S.Borges/
https://www.instagram.com/rebeccaborges1
https://www.instagram.com/liveplanthappy
https://www.linkedin.com/in/rebecca-borges/

The Strength of Being Different: My Journey from Outsider to Innovator

Antonette Carabuena

I was born in the Philippines and grew up in Holyoke, Mass., as part of a hard-working immigrant family. From a young age, I understood what it meant to be different. My skin color, my Filipino accent, and the lunches I brought to gatherings, events, and class—adobo, rice, and sometimes lumpia—set me apart. I faced judgment, not just from peers but from a world that often made me feel like an outsider.

My mother raised four children alone, working double shifts as a Filipino nurse in America to send us to private school and provide the best life she never had. She is my hero—the definition of strength and sacrifice.

Growing up, my siblings were my closest friends. No matter how much I was judged by bullies, I knew I had a support system at home. My *lola* (grandma) also taught me to care and share, but to never let anyone take advantage of me. These values shaped my identity and my resilience.

In college, nursing was not my first choice. I always wanted a career that was in business, one that utilized creativity and innovation. However, my path led me to nursing, where I found a way to integrate my passion for leadership and problem-solving with the ability to make a real impact on people's lives.

Now, as a nurse and entrepreneur, I carry these lessons forward. My mission is to transform nursing—to create a space where nurses are valued and to redefine the quality of patient care. Because being different doesn't mean being lesser—it means having the power to make a difference.

The Heroes in Scrubs: A Tribute to My Roots

Nurses are the silent warriors of healthcare, standing on the front lines, giving everything they have to their patients, often at the expense of their own well-being. They are the first to hold a trembling hand, the first to offer comfort in moments of despair, and the last to leave the bedside when hope is slipping away. Yet, despite their sacrifice, they are often unseen, unappreciated, and overworked.

I grew up watching one of these warriors—my mother. A Filipino nurse who worked tirelessly, taking double shifts just to make sure her children had a chance at a better life. I remember waiting by the door late at night, hoping to catch a glimpse of her before she collapsed into bed. Her uniform carried the scent of antiseptic and the weight of long, exhausting hours. Her feet ached, her hands were worn, yet she never let us see her pain. She wore her resilience like armor, her compassion like a guiding light.

One night, I saw her sitting alone at the kitchen table, rubbing her temples, exhaustion evident in every breath she took. I quietly sat beside her, hoping she would say something, but instead, she just smiled at me. A soft, tired smile—the kind that only a mother can give, the kind that says, *Everything is okay, even when it isn't.* That moment stayed with me. It was in that silence that I saw her strength. Not just the strength of a nurse, but the strength of a mother who gave everything for her children.

Filipino nurses like my mother have become the backbone of healthcare systems around the world. They carry with them not only skill but an unmatched level of care, treating patients as if they were family. I have seen this firsthand—the way they hold a patient's hand a little longer, the way they remember every small detail about them, the way they go beyond what is required, because to them, nursing is not just a job. It is a calling.

It is in our roots to be compassionate, to heal, to nurture. But it is also in our roots to endure, to fight, and to rise. I have inherited this from my mother. The unwavering commitment to serve, the quiet strength in adversity, and the relentless spirit to push forward despite the odds.

I am proud to be the daughter of a Filipino nurse. And I am proud to stand among them today—not just as a nurse, but as an advocate for change. I carry my mother's legacy with me in every patient I care for, in every decision I make, and in every step I take toward reshaping the nursing profession. This is my tribute—not just to her, but to every nurse who has sacrificed, who has endured, and who continues to be the unsung hero of healthcare.

Being Seen, Being Judged

Being different is being seen. But being seen doesn't always mean being accepted. I learned this early in life, growing up in Massachusetts as a Filipino immigrant. I was short, I had an accent, my skin was darker than anyone in the room, and the food I brought for lunch—warm adobo, fluffy rice, and sometimes crispy lumpia—made me an easy target for ridicule.

I remember sitting in the cafeteria, opening my lunchbox with excitement, only to hear the laughter and whispers. "*What is that smell?*" someone would say, scrunching their nose. I felt a sting of shame, not because I disliked my food, but because at that moment, I felt like an outsider. Like I didn't belong.

With any interaction, my accent made me hesitant to speak up. My size made me easy to pick on. My skin, my culture, my entire existence felt like something I had to defend. But at home, I never felt small.

Bullies are cowards. They prey on those they think they can underestimate, but they were wrong about me. I fought, I stood up, and I was fierce. I caught them off guard. The envious, the jealous, the bullies—they lost, not because I fought them physically, but because I let success be my noise.

My mother, my greatest role model, was always working—double jobs, endless shifts—to give us more than what she had growing up. She worked tirelessly to support four children on her own. Even with little, she made us feel like we had everything. My father, though not as present, left me with words that have guided me to this day: *If they don't invite you to their table, build your own.*

I didn't realize it then, but those lessons—of resilience, of confidence, of knowing my worth—would shape my entire journey.

Finding My Path in Nursing

I was never the smartest among my four siblings. They were honor students, top of their class, and naturally gifted. I, on the other hand, had to work twice as hard just to keep up. I wasn't exceptional at one particular thing, but I was determined. My mother called me the *jack of all trades*, someone who could adapt to anything. And she was right. I had grit. I was ambidextrous. And no matter how many times I was told, "You can't," I always found a way.

When I chose nursing, I knew it wouldn't be easy. Back then, landing a nursing job wasn't as simple as it is today. I faced rejection after rejection. I wasn't the first choice, not because I lacked the skills, but because sometimes the world judges you before you even get a chance to prove yourself.

But perseverance paid off. I became a critical care nurse, a career that demanded everything—mental, emotional, and physical strength. I worked long shifts, made life-or-death decisions, and carried the emotional weight of patients and their families. And yet, despite all of this, nurses were often reduced to a stereotype: someone to fetch ginger ale, someone to clean up a mess.

It was frustrating. We were the backbone of healthcare, but we were often overlooked. Still, I pushed forward, knowing that I was meant to be in this profession.

And then, COVID-19 happened.

The Breaking Point

The pandemic changed everything. Hospitals were overwhelmed. Nurses were overworked, underappreciated, and breaking down. I watched some of the most compassionate, intelligent nurses leave the profession—not because they didn't love nursing, but because the system had drained them completely.

Burnout became an epidemic of its own. Nurses worked shifts so long that they barely had time to sleep. They skipped meals, ignored their own health, and sacrificed everything for their patients. But no one was taking care of them.

I saw the problem firsthand: nurses were being treated as disposable, and patient care was suffering as a result.

That's when I remembered my father's words: *Build your own table.*

If the system wasn't going to change, I would create a solution.

Creating Curantis: A New Vision for Nursing

That's when I founded Curantis Private Nursing Services—a luxury concierge nursing company designed to solve two major problems: burnout among nurses and declining patient care.

In a private, one-on-one setting, nurses can focus on quality over quantity. They can provide personalized, top-tier care without the stress of hospital politics, understaffed units, and overwhelming caseloads. And most importantly, they can be treated as the skilled professionals they are—valued, respected, and fairly compensated.

Curantis isn't just about private nursing. It's about shifting the way the world sees nurses.

Nurses are not just assistants. They are decision-makers. They are advocates. They are healers. And they deserve to work in an environment where their skills and expertise are appreciated.

Through Curantis, I am proving that there is another way. That nurses don't have to settle for burnout. That patients don't have to receive subpar care.

At Curantis, we believe in transforming the nursing experience—not only for the patients but for the nurses who dedicate their lives to this field. Our model is built on the understanding that nursing care should be personal, compassionate, and focused on well-being rather than administrative burdens. By offering a supportive work environment, flexible scheduling, and a premium standard of care, we are not only preventing burnout but elevating the profession as a whole.

Curantis stands as a beacon of change, demonstrating that nurses deserve a career where their expertise is honored, where they are not just employees but partners in healthcare and nursing excellence. Patients are not just numbers; they are individuals deserving of customized, quality care. This is the future of nursing—one where nurses have control over their schedules, where their professional growth is prioritized, and where patients receive an elevated experience that fosters trust and healing.

We are redefining nursing beyond traditional hospital walls, creating an ecosystem that values both the nurse and the patient, ensuring that compassionate care is not rushed but deeply intentional.

A Mission Bigger Than Myself

When I look back at my journey, from the bullied immigrant kid in Massachusetts to a nurse entrepreneur leading change—I see one common thread: resilience.

I was never given a seat at the table, so I built my own.

I was told I was different, and I made that my strength.

I faced rejection, and I turned it into motivation.

Now, my mission is clear: I want to make nursing sustainable. I want to give nurses a reason to stay in the profession they love. I want to redefine what high-quality patient care looks like.

Most importantly, I want to show the next generation of nurses—especially those who feel different, unseen, and underestimated—that they, too, can create their own path.

Because being different doesn't mean being lesser. It means having the power to change the world.

About the Author

Antonette was born in the Philippines and raised in Holyoke, Mass., as part of a resilient immigrant family. From a young age, she knew what it felt like to be different. Her brown skin, Filipino accent, and the adobo and lumpia in her lunchbox set her apart in classrooms and gatherings. The world didn't always understand her—but that only fueled her desire to create her own path.

Antonette's mother, a Filipino nurse working double shifts to raise four children alone, is her greatest hero. Despite her sacrifices, she made sure Antonette never felt she lacked anything. Antonette's father, though not always present, taught her something equally powerful: if you're not invited to the table, build your own.

Antonette grew up with her siblings as her closest friends and her lola's (grandmother's) wisdom in her heart: give freely, love fully, but never compromise your worth. These values grounded her.

Though Antonette initially dreamed of a business career, she found her calling in nursing. There, she discovered how to blend creativity, leadership, and compassion into something truly transformational. Today, she is the founder of Curantis Private Nursing Services, a luxury concierge private nursing company.

As a nurse entrepreneur with over fifteen years of clinical experience and a master's degree in nursing administration, she is committed to elevating the standard of patient care and empowering nurses to see themselves as leaders and innovators.

Being different is no longer her challenge—it's her superpower. And Antonette intends to use it to rewrite the narrative of what's possible for nurses, immigrants, and anyone daring to dream beyond the norm.

https://curantisnursing.com

The Courage to Be Unapologetically You

Gabriella Celona

This chapter is dedicated to my mom (for always wanting what's best for me), and my nana and grandpa, Linda and Louis Fronduto. Life isn't the same without you. I wouldn't be anywhere without your love and support.

I am very excited to introduce myself. My name is Gabriella Celona. I am a twenty-three-year-old from Boston, Mass. I grew up about ten minutes outside of the city with my mom, my two younger sisters Alexandra and Guilianna, and my nana and grandpa.

The first thing you should know about me is that I am extremely family-oriented. My family means everything and more to me. I would quite literally do anything for any of them.

My mom, as a single mother, raised us, her three daughters. Right from the start, I had a strong woman figure in my life. My mom worked three jobs to provide for us. My grandparents served as an extension of my mom—kind of like extended parents, you could say. I was very close with my grandparents. I saw the dynamic my mom had with her parents, which obviously trickled down to the rest of us being exceptionally tight-knit. I would do anything to have Sunday dinners with my grandparents here again, to call my nana in the morning to debrief my night after I went to a college party, and to sing "oldies but goodies" tracks with my grandpa.

Let's rewind back to about thirteen years ago. My dad passed away a week before my eleventh birthday. I didn't live with my dad growing up. Only when I was younger, up until I was about six. I don't remember much about living together, but I do have a good chunk of memories of him.

It's disheartening to see three young girls lose their father at such a young age. But you have to look at situations like these in a different light. I look at it as a gift rather than a loss; although my dad passed away and I do wonder what my relationship with him would be at my age now, I got to live with three parental figures—my mom, my nana, and my grandpa.

If you were to ask me, I would have never known my mom was ever struggling. I had a great childhood. I danced growing up (a very expensive passion to choose), and my sisters played baseball and did cheerleading. We consistently went on vacations, especially to Disney World. We have lived a great life and were just as spoiled as all the other kids, if not more; but above all of that, we receive so much love. Love and a strong family dynamic is as rich as you can get.

Ever since I was a kid, I've been drawn to the entertainment world. My personality shined right through as soon as I took my first step into a dance class. I was immediately a natural performer, a star. Dance was my first ever love. Not only was it my first love, but it continues to be the love of my life. Technically, I've been dancing since age one, a week before my second birthday. Being on stage and in front of a crowd is a feeling that I could never get anywhere else. Dance is not only a passion or hobby of mine; I train very hard to be able to say that I am a professional dancer. I have worked on projects like live concerts, worked with brands like New Balance, performed at the Celtics NBA games, and more. I am trained in ballet, contemporary, jazz, jazz funk, hip-hop, modern dance (specifically the Horton Technique), heels dance, and more. I work with the best teachers in the city.

I'm not going to shy away from saying I like to be the center of attention—it's true, but it's not that I think I'm better than anyone. I just have such a love for what I am doing that I shine when I'm on stage—I catch your eye, and I can feel that. I have personality, flavor, and I feel the artistry, movement and musicality of what dance is, regardless of what style I'm dancing to. I have a deep appreciation for the craft, for my mentors, and I have the discipline to insert myself into that world. You could be the best dancer at your studio, but you go to an audition in another state, and there will always be someone better. That fire fuels me to train harder. I go to the front in a master class because I want to be attentive and present in the class, and that's where I learn best. When in a dance class, I want to stand next to the best dancer in the room so I can push myself to be a better version of myself. When dancing, I *feel* the music, I *feel* every movement, and I become very present in my body, connecting to my heart, my soul, and the infinite expression of who I am.

I love the creative space. My chosen high school extracurricular class was studying film and media. Some people took it for fun, and others took it in hopes of pursuing it as a career. As the years went on, I took all four levels of the class. We worked on creating, advertising, editing, and dissecting films, music videos, and anything else you can think of in this realm. I spent morning, noon, and night working in that classroom whenever I wasn't in my other academic classes. During my junior year of high school, my media teacher decided that we should start broadcasting morning announcements. I immediately thought to myself, *I would love to do that*! I loved the creative space of film and television, but I know I preferred being in front of the camera, just like I loved being on stage. I was the first ever Malden High School student to broadcast the school's daily news. This is when I began to understand exactly what I wanted to do: report for entertainment, attend red carpet events, and interview people who ultimately love the same things that I do.

Although I did want to go further away for college, I ended up attending Emerson College in Boston. It was the perfect school for what I wanted to do. I know now that everything truly does happen for a reason because I was able to make even more memories with my grandparents during their last years.

I graduated high school and started college in the midst of the pandemic, so my first year was good but very different from the traditional freshman year away from home. We had a hybrid model schedule and had to wear masks everywhere. The dining hall was take-out only, and we had to get tested for COVID twice a week or else we weren't allowed to go to class or even get into our dorm rooms. I met a decent amount of people because all of us freshmen were in the same building, but there were so many restrictions that it was hard to meet new people other than those who were in our classes or on our dorm floors.

Luckily, my sophomore year was significantly more quintessential. I met so many new people. It was like what you'd expect in a typical first year in college: parties every weekend and plenty of other opportunities to mingle. Community has always been important to me, so I joined one of the school's dance crews where I was on A-board for the contemporary company, along with trying to attend and support the rest of the sporting events at the school. I love the sports environment. This may have sprung from how Bostonians are sports fanatics, but I genuinely love the way it brings people together to have a good time. We represent Boston as a whole, as a community. Although Emerson isn't necessarily *known* for their sports, I went to almost any game I could attend, and we had a pretty cool group we hung out with. You gotta support your team... am I right?

While attending Emerson, I was one of the only people in my major who took less of a traditional route in the broadcasting department. On my own, I went out and made connections within the Boston area; I reached out to different magazines and attended events to do red-carpet-type interviews. I covered so many events in Massachusetts and met so many people by doing this, I started to make a name for myself. I applied for an internship with *AfterBuzz TV* based out of Los Angeles to make more connections. In my junior year of college, I attended New York Fashion Week with WEBN news, but the shows I went to with my crew just weren't enough for me. I ended up having a connection from Boston that happened to be working for the Jovani fashion show. What do you know... I found myself attending a huge event in New York City, and I did it all by myself, again. When opportunities come, you need to jump on them. The Mr. Martinis company saw me working at a magazine launch and loved what I was doing, so I became the one and only Princess Martini. I hosted the event, did promotional videos leading up to the event, and interviewed amidst chaos during the competition. I was the face of the company.

I went to another event to perform my choreography and ended up getting hired for social media and event planning at

Advanced Addiction Center and Advanced Therapy Center, a fast-growing company. How did I make this happen? I just asked! I put myself out there. The owner of the company had seen my work and my passion, so they hired me. I am able to push boundaries within my work and bring awareness to a cause I deeply care about, which is mental health. I now have the company's support to put on an event in honor of my grandparents, where all the proceeds are going to lung cancer research.

I am in no way saying that going to college didn't teach me anything; I am saying that regardless of what I studied in school, I just go for what I want and make it happen because I know I can.

I asked my sisters how they would describe me, and let me tell you, my sisters are my biggest critics and my biggest supporters, so they will hurt my feelings if need be. Luckily, their response was, "Extremely outgoing, loving, personable, loud, and caring."

Along with these adjectives, I would also say I am a pretty confrontational person. Now listen, people hear the word "confrontational" and immediately have a negative connotation, when it's not always a negative thing. For example, I personally like to deal with things head-on, and although that may be hard for other people, I want to address the problem at the root of the situation, rather than letting resentment or whatever build up over time. I am confrontational because I would rather hash whatever it is out right away than have other people talking about my business.

I am *A. Drama. Queen*. Dramatic can often be perceived as inauthentic or attention seeking, when, in my case, it couldn't be more opposite. I am dramatic in the way that I *feel* everything. I am very in-tune with my emotions. When I'm happy, I am over-the-moon happy; when I am sad, I am so so sad. It's hard for me to feel anything in between. When I'm happy, I cry, when I'm sad, I cry, and when I'm mad, I could also cry. I can quite literally cry over EVERYTHING. (Funny enough, even as a performer, if you were to ask me to cry on command, I wouldn't be able to do it.)

If you were to ask me to describe myself, I would pretty much agree with what my sisters said and add fun, energetic, and fabulous (when I want to be, haha). But whether these traits put me in great situations or devastating ones, I would say my personality is the best thing about me. It's why I've accomplished so many things at such a young age.

Lean into your personality. Lean into the things you want for yourself, even if they seem scary. For me, if I'm wary about something, more often than not, I go for it rather than taking a back seat. And although that comes naturally to me, I truly want to encourage anyone making big decisions to just do it. Do something crazy like moving across the country to pursue your passions. Do what makes you happy! Everything else will fall into place.

I live my life carefree, so when it comes to my life I say, "I don't care what random people have to say because it's my life, and it makes me happy." While I do have this attitude, I am also an empath. I care more about other people's feelings than my own, and I care a lot more about situations and certain people than I should, which is a boundary I personally need to continue to work on within myself.

I always remember something my good friend Julia once said to me. We became close after high school, but during high school, we kind of crossed paths because we hung out with similar people. She said, "Gab, people who talk shit about you and say you're fake are just envious because you're so real. People don't believe that you're being genuine when you really are, because not a lot of people are like that anymore." Honestly, this really stuck with me; I know that I have been nothing but genuine with all of my relationships in my life, but it was nice to finally hear it from an outside perspective, from someone I wasn't very close with at the time but who is now in my inner circle for a reason.

I am very straightforward. I like to say I would treat the person on the side of the street as I would my best friend, although this is not a great personality trait for me because I end up getting hurt a lot of the time.

As you've probably gathered, to say it plain and simple: I am an extrovert. While this is true, I grew up struggling with a severe anxiety disorder. I would say that the only one I do not have is social anxiety, because that's where I thrive. I am and have always been very open about mental health, and do everything I can to help others who struggle. I want people to trust me when opening up about their experiences. It's personal, and it hits deep. Mental health disorders can be caused by genetics, life experiences, and/or one's environment. There are many factors that go into this.

Now, I am going to say something that might rub people the wrong way and honestly, I don't care. Having a hard day or two DOES NOT mean you have a mental health disorder. Let me say it again: being "sad" is not the same thing as being depressed; being "organized" does not mean you have OCD; feeling "stressed" does not mean you have an anxiety disorder, and so on. Although these are some common effects of mental health disorders, so much more goes into play. While it's amazing how awareness of mental health issues has grown, it is also extremely disrespectful for people to use mental health as an excuse when there are people who can't live their lives normally because of the struggles a real mental health disorder brings.

Right now I am at the point in my life where I just graduated college and am starting my real adult life. I've heard the stories of how people become super depressed once they graduate college because they don't know what's next. I wouldn't say I am in the position of not knowing what's next, but I do feel a little stuck because I am in the process of navigating my path in the real world. The entertainment industry is a lion within itself—

but especially in this economy, there are more layoffs than ever before. Entertainment companies are letting loyal, longtime employees go, and influencers are taking our jobs. I have so much respect for influencers, and I think what they do can be super beneficial. But at the same time, it doesn't seem fair that influencers can get a reporting job over a trained journalist just because of their social media presence. My brand has a lot of similarities with the things that influencers do, so I am in absolutely no way saying anything negative about them. What I am saying is that it's harder than ever right now for people trying to break into the industry, regardless of what area of entertainment you're trying to break into.

I am a go-getter, enthusiastic, a lover of everything and everyone. I always want to see others do well. One thing I've unfortunately noticed in the entertainment industry is that everyone just worries about themselves because everyone's fighting for the same thing—and people will play dirty to get it. I knew from the jump that was going to be something I needed to be aware of because I am way too trusting of others and I have a habit of just assuming everyone is trying to be nice. Although this is one of my great traits, it can bite me in the ass at times. I expect everyone to be authentic all the time, because that's how I live my life; but time and time again, I come to the realization that that's not how life works, no matter how much you want it to.

Find good people who help you stay creative, who don't judge you, and who actually want to see you succeed.

I decided to create my own entertainment media company called "The Gift To Gab," where I show my bubbly personality through the realm of multimedia platforms and content.

I think my brand was formed long ago—I just needed to slap a name on it.

Many people view social media as a negative space, often labeling it as fake or superficial. However, for me, social media has always been a platform to express my authentic self and showcase my true personality. It's a tool to connect with others, build a community, and encourage people to embrace who they are—to be free, fun, and unapologetically themselves. I believe in using social media to celebrate realness, creativity, and genuine connections.

Starting a company is hard; it's not something everyone wants to do, and it comes with a lot more work and responsibilities than you necessarily want to do or expect. I originally decided to start my own company because: one, the industry is not consistent with hiring and keeping people on; two, I wanted to continue to create good quality content; and three, I wanted my content to be organized well under a specific brand. My brand is basically my personality in a nutshell. This is honestly great for me, considering I do think a lot about how the industry is constantly changing; content now is very different from what millennials are used to, and content Gen Z has is a whole new way of thinking.

I try to stay curious about where the fine line is between what is "acceptable" in the workplace and what isn't. For instance, I wonder what the people hiring me will say when my content is a little more personable, like what the new generation engages with, rather than traditional professional content. The concept of professionalism is relative; just because the newer generation does things differently and has more of an open-minded way of thinking, does not mean it's not considered professional. Content is always changing, but that is why I wanted to create my own company, so I can create content the way I want, while also relaying fun, engaging information about the entertainment world.

As I said earlier I am not a "traditional news" type of girl. I'm too much fun for that. I like to combine the idea of entertainment news with the mindset of this generation and add what's trending in the media.

Over the years, my personality literally has not changed. I've evolved, grown up, and been through more shit as time goes on, but my heart remains in the same place after it all. And that's what gets me ahead of others and is where my ambition comes from: my authenticity. I don't compete with anyone in a nasty way; I focus more on my own projects than what other people are doing, and I enjoy life.

About the Author

Gabriella Celona is a dynamic reporter, producer, and multifaceted talent who thrives in the worlds of lifestyle, entertainment, and performance. With a keen eye for social media and an undeniable on-screen presence, Gabriella brings her vibrant, bubbly, and energetic personality to everything she does. She doesn't just stop there; she is also a professional dancer, seamlessly blending her love for movement, creativity, and passion. Gabriella values every connection she makes, and takes it as an opportunity to uplift others. For her, community is not just about sharing experiences, it is about coming together as a whole, working as a team, and striving for something bigger than ourselves.

Ultimately, Gabriella is a beacon of empowerment, inspiring others to live boldly and authentically. Her motto is, *"Who cares what other people think? It's your life. Do what makes you happy!"* Her authenticity and unwavering commitment to doing what feels right for her is a constant reminder that true happiness lies in embracing one's most genuine self. Through her projects, Gabriella leads by example, showing that when you live unapologetically, you get further in life, and you inspire others to do the same.

www.gabriellacelona.com
https://www.instagram.com/gabriellacelona/
https://www.instagram.com/thegifttogab/
https://www.tiktok.com/@gabriella.celona

From Operating Rooms to Grazing Tables: A Story of Healing and Creation

Robyn Daigle

Brie Awesome & Stay Cheesy...

Yeah, I know, it's a bit of a head-turner. It makes you smile, right? That's the point. It's more than just a tagline, though. It's the vibe, the whole damn point of what I'm building. It's about finding joy even when life throws you a curveball—or in my case, a fastball.

People look at me now, building charcuterie boards and grazing tables, and they say, "Wow, you're so lucky to do what you love." And I get it. From the outside, it looks like a dream. But "lucky" doesn't even begin to cover the journey. It's been a wild ride—a rollercoaster of fear, pain, and ultimately, a whole lot of resilience.

February 15, 2022. That's when everything changed. I finished work and went to pick up my sweet mini-Labradoodle, Napa, from daycare when suddenly, my left arm felt tight. I brushed it off, thinking it was caused by something as simple as my sweater bunched up in my jacket. But the pain rapidly worsened. When I asked my husband if my arm looked weird, the look on his face was like he had seen a ghost. Next thing I know, I'm alone in the emergency room, COVID rules keeping visitors to a minimum. My arm turned purple, totally numb, and ice cold. My first thought? "Okay, I'm losing my arm."

Hours later, my mom joined me in the hospital, and an ultrasound tech walked in with a look that could turn blood to ice as the on-call surgeon dropped the bomb: thoracic outlet syndrome. "It's rare," he said. "Just don't Google it." He told me that all the veins in my left arm, from my wrist to my shoulder, were completely clotted. Immediately, a million questions flooded my mind.

That first night was a blur. My mom was crying, I was trying to comfort her, and I had to relay this nightmare to my husband. I was in a room with three other patients and a blaring TV, but I just sat there alone with my thoughts. What was this? What did it mean for my life? For my husband? Would I still be able to do the things I was passionate about? I needed to cry, but I forced myself to stay strong.

The next morning, the surgeon came in to meet with me. He was a beacon of calm in the chaos. He confirmed the diagnosis and laid out the plan: three surgeries, a long recovery, no guarantees. The first would be an angiogram, where they would go into my arm and remove all of the blood clots. The second was a first rib resection, a surgery to remove my first rib. The third and final surgery was a venogram to remove any additional blood clots that may have lingered from the past surgeries. He drew diagrams on a whiteboard, explaining the mess inside my body. He gave me tissues, and I finally let the tears flow. It wasn't just the diagnosis; it was the sheer vulnerability of it all.

For five days I had an IV of blood thinners, my arm swollen like a balloon, and a pain that made me want to scream. My right arm, which had become a pin cushion for blood draws, finally stopped giving blood—who knew this could happen! And then it was surgery day. I waited all day, no food, no water, just the gnawing pain and the fear of what was to come.

Honestly, how did it feel waking up from that angiogram? To this day, it is still the scariest thing I have gone through. I was not just holding onto my husband's hands, but *gripping* them, as tears were streaming down my face. I was begging him not to let go, because I genuinely thought if I closed my eyes I wouldn't wake up again. And then, as my heart felt like it was going haywire, with my blood pressure plummeting then rising, then plummeting again, the doctors told him he had to leave. Just like that. I was terrified.

The next day I was a mess. I was in the worst pain of my life. But I pushed through. I fought to do the walking exercises and move from the bed to the chair—which took everything out of me. By seven p.m that night, I was home. My husband, my friends, my village, they were all there for me. My "new normal" was a cocktail of pain meds, blood thinners, and a whole lot of vulnerability. My husband bathed me, brushed my hair, and cut my food. I couldn't lift my arm.

A few weeks later, I had my second surgery to remove my first rib. I learned of the complications after the surgery, alongside the surgeon's vivid description: "It was like scraping concrete off your nerves." My arm felt both numb and burning, a sensation that wouldn't leave for years. That recovery was truly hell. I was confined to a recliner in my living room, unable to move without help. My arm was always wrapped in compression, and I had to fall asleep surrounded by ice and heat; it was an experience I wouldn't wish on anyone. I had two months of solitude in that chair, just me, Netflix, and my racing thoughts. For the first time in my life, I was forced into complete inactivity. At twenty-nine years old, my life had been irrevocably changed, and I had to figure out what came next. *Life's too short to be unhappy*, I told myself, clinging to hope.

A month later, I had the third and final surgery, the venogram, and though I was medically cleared, I was still in pain and still struggling. Depression hit hard. I sought help, started medication, and I slowly found my way toward healing.

But what now? Corporate life wasn't working. I needed to put myself first. So, I quit. I had no backup plan, just a gut feeling. I needed to rediscover myself, to rebuild my strength, and to re-teach my arm how to do everything. "What makes me truly happy?" I asked myself. I kept coming back to my passion for helping people. But how could I do that? Then the holidays rolled around, and my friends started raving about my charcuterie boards. "Sell these!" they said. "You have a business!" At first, I laughed. But then I thought about it more. I could create a business that prioritized my mental and physical health. I could work for myself, help others, and give myself the therapy I needed. My village pushed me, reminding me of my Bentley education and the support I had. "What's the worst that can happen?" they asked. "If it doesn't work, at least you tried."

It was like that moment when you receive a compliment, and you finally have the confidence to believe it. I took the leap and started Boards for Days. Charcuterie, yes, but also anything I wanted to create. "For days" meant celebrating every single day with new creations.

After everything I had been through, I was ready to try anything. Entrepreneur life isn't glamorous. It's hard work, long hours, and a constant struggle for balance. But it's also gratitude, appreciation, and a deep respect for myself.

I'm a badass woman who sets big goals and achieves them. I have been featured on CBS and published in *Better Homes & Garden*. I have a growing team, and we are booked through the weekends to help people celebrate special occasions. I am helping people; I am doing the damn thing.

"You're not faking it until you make it," a wise woman once told me. "You're making it every damn day." And she was right.

As I look forward, I embrace my resilience, my intuition, my story. We're all capable of more than we think. This journey is hard, but it's worth it. Every day, I strive to be the best version of myself. Some days are easy, some days are a struggle. But I always remember how I got here. I've faced the pain, and now it's time to live. Be bold, be kind, be you.

Brie Awesome & Stay Cheesy,

Robyn

About the Author

Robyn, owner of Boards for Days, is a charcuterie expert and entrepreneur who believes in turning life's challenges into opportunities. After a rare medical condition changed her life in 2022, she channeled her passion for food and relationships into a thriving business, prioritizing mental and physical well-being. Featured on CBS and in *Better Homes & Garden*, Robyn's "Brie Awesome & Stay Cheesy" philosophy is a testament to her belief in living life to the fullest. This chapter shares her journey from pain to purpose, offering readers a raw and honest look at resilience, entrepreneurship, and the power of food to bring people together.

www.boardsfordays.com

Instagram: @boardsfordays_

Justice with a Heart

Morjieta Derisier

As the daughter of Haitian immigrants, my journey into the legal profession has been profoundly influenced by my heritage and the experiences of my family. My parents' resilience and determination in the face of adversity instilled in me a deep commitment to justice and advocacy.

Growing up, I was acutely aware of the challenges faced by the Haitian community in the United States. My parents often shared stories of their struggles to navigate a new culture, confront discrimination, and establish a stable life for our family. One particularly poignant experience involved a close family friend who was wrongfully accused of a crime due to racial profiling. Witnessing his ordeal—the stigma, loss of livelihood, and emotional toll—ignited a fire within me to stand up for those who couldn't defend themselves. This experience cemented my belief that everyone deserves fair representation, a cornerstone of our legal system.

At the heart of defense law is the ability to connect genuinely with clients. Each individual who walks into my office carries a unique story, often marred by fear, regret, or confusion. It's imperative to listen without judgment, to understand their journey, and to provide a beacon of hope amidst the tumult.

I recall a case where a young Haitian immigrant was charged with a serious offense. Beyond the legal implications, he grappled with societal judgment and personal guilt. By establishing a genuine connection, we navigated the legal challenges together, addressing not just the case but his holistic well-being. This approach not only aids in building a robust defense but also ensures that clients feel valued and understood.

The Reality of Defense Law: Beyond Monetary Gains

A common misconception is that practicing law equates to substantial wealth. While some legal avenues may lead to financial prosperity, defense law is often driven by passion rather than profit. The cases undertaken frequently involve individuals from marginalized communities who lack the resources for hefty legal fees. The reward, therefore, isn't monetary; instead it's about the profound satisfaction of upholding justice.

Transparency about the financial aspects is crucial. There are months when the overheads surpass the income, especially when taking on pro bono cases or those with minimal remuneration. Yet, the commitment to making a difference keeps the journey worthwhile.

The daily life of a defense attorney is anything but monotonous. Mornings often begin with client meetings, understanding their narratives, and gathering facts. Afternoons are reserved for court appearances, presenting motions, or negotiating plea deals. Evenings might involve meticulous research, reviewing case laws, and strategizing for upcoming trials.

For instance, a typical day might start with a jail visit to a client, followed by drafting legal documents, and culminating in a court hearing that extends late into the evening. The unpredictability is a constant, requiring adaptability and resilience.

Each case leaves an indelible mark, teaching lessons and shaping the attorney-client relationship.

One of the most poignant heartbreaks of mine involved defending a young man accused of a crime he didn't commit. Despite presenting compelling evidence of his innocence, biases and systemic flaws led to his conviction. The devastation of witnessing an innocent person incarcerated is immeasurable, underscoring the imperfections within the justice system.

Yet there are many moments of profound triumph. I recall a case where a client facing severe charges was acquitted after a relentless pursuit of truth. The gratitude in his eyes and his family's deep relief served as a powerful reminder of why I chose this path.

As defense attorneys, we are but guides in our clients' journeys. The focus should always remain on their narratives, ensuring that their voices are amplified, and their rights protected. This client-centric approach fosters trust and leads to more effective representation.

In my work, I use an approach which we refer to as "active fluffy law"—some people see this as ineffective but to me it represents a balance of empathy and objectivity. The term "active fluffy law" might evoke images of a lenient or overly empathetic approach. However, in practice, it signifies balancing empathy with objectivity. It's about understanding the human element in each case while rigorously applying legal principles. This balance ensures that while clients feel supported, the integrity of the legal process remains intact.

Leaving Your Mark

Leaving a mark as a defense attorney isn't about high-profile cases or public accolades. It's about the silent victories—the teenager given a second chance, the wrongfully accused exonerated, the families reunited. It's about challenging systemic injustices and advocating for reforms. The true legacy lies in the lives touched and the justice served.

The path of a defense attorney is laden with challenges, but it's a journey of profound significance. By connecting genuinely with clients, understanding the true essence of the profession beyond monetary gains, navigating daily complexities, and embracing both heartbreaks and successes, one can leave an indelible mark on the tapestry of justice. This legacy isn't etched in statutes or legal times but in the hearts of those we've had the privilege to defend.

About the Author

Morjieta Derisier, Esq. is an accomplished attorney, legal analyst, and entrepreneur who has dedicated her career to justice, advocacy, and community empowerment. As a featured legal analyst for NBC10 Boston, she provides expert commentary on high-profile criminal cases, offering clear and insightful legal perspectives to a broad audience.

With over twelve years of litigation experience, Morjieta is the co-owner of Baystate Law Group PLLC, where she represents clients in criminal defense, real estate law, and business litigation. Her sharp legal acumen and unwavering commitment to fairness have earned her numerous accolades, including but not limited to the 2024 Top Women of Law by *Massachusetts Lawyers Weekly,* 2024 Top Criminal Defense Attorney by *Boston Magazine,* and the 2025 Suffolk University Celebration of Black Excellence Outstanding Alumni for the College of Arts and Sciences.

In addition to her legal practice, Morjieta is deeply committed to mentorship and advocacy. She serves as a mentor for Suffolk Lawyers for Justice, guiding and supporting attorneys in their criminal defense work. She is also in the process of launching an initiative designed to empower women by providing the tools, resources, and strategies to build successful businesses and advocate for themselves in legal and professional spaces.

www.jietad.com

All in on Me: The Ultimate Gamble of Self-Investment

Dede Forgione

From the moment I was born, I knew I was different. Growing up as one of the only Italian families in a tight-knit Jewish community, I always felt like an outsider, navigating a world that didn't quite understand me. I was the girl who stood out in ways that weren't always easy to embrace, one of the only "chunky" girls in a world of slender Barbies. I was mocked, ridiculed, and bullied by other children who found joy in hurting someone like me. This cruelty didn't just sting; it cut deep, leaving scars I didn't fully understand at the time. But even in those dark moments, I had something most people didn't: an unshakable love and support from my family.

Every day, no matter how cruel the world outside my door felt, I came home to a fortress of love. My family's unwavering support was the one thing that kept me going. No matter what happened, I was always welcomed home with open arms, a warm hug, and words of encouragement that lifted my spirit. I learned early on that strength wasn't about how you looked or what others said about you—it was about the love and resilience that radiated from within. My family taught me that, and that love became the foundation for everything I would endure in the years to come.

When I was eighteen, my life was shattered by the loss of my mother, my angel. I'll never forget the moment she passed. The grief was suffocating, but in the midst of that heartbreak, something shifted in me. I had to grow up fast. My childhood was ripped away, and I was forced to step into shoes I wasn't ready for. But I didn't have a choice. My family needed me. My mother's illness kept me tethered to home, and college—a dream I had worked for—became an impossible luxury. I wasn't expected to stay home; I chose to stay home because I felt obligated to try to hold the pieces of our family together. Every day, I sacrificed a part of myself, learning what it meant to be a woman, a caretaker, and a pillar of strength.

The grief that followed my mother's death felt like I was drowning, struggling to keep my head above water. But as if life wasn't already cruel enough, I watched my father slowly slip away from us, swept up in a new relationship that drove a wedge between us all. It felt like everything was falling apart, but in those darkest moments, my brother became my rock. He stood by me and helped to support me. He was in college when our mom passed away, but he took me under his wing and looked out for me. His brilliance in the medical field encouraged me to push forward, even when I felt completely lost. He gave me hope, showing me that there was still something worth fighting for.

I thought I had found a break when I landed a job working in the elections division for the secretary of the Commonwealth. Starting from the bottom, I worked tirelessly, learning everything I could about how our democracy functioned. I earned promotions, moving up the ranks and excelling beyond my wildest expectations. I was then approached by a large city here in Massachusetts and poached to become the deputy director of their elections division. It was a dream-come-true; I had stability for the first time since childhood. But just when I thought I was on solid ground, everything changed. A shift in mayoral leadership left me with a severance package, and suddenly, I was back at square one.

But the blows didn't stop coming. Alongside losing my job, I found myself trapped in a toxic relationship with a narcissist. This man didn't just walk in and out of my life—he weaved in and out for fifteen long years, draining me emotionally, mentally, and spiritually. No matter how many times I tried to move on, he would reappear, taking and taking, never giving anything back. I spent years riding the emotional roller coaster with him, hoping things would change, but they never did. He never added any value to my life—he simply took. And after everything I had already lost, he took the one thing I could never get back: the chance to become a mother. With every cycle of heartbreak and abandonment, I lost precious years, watching my childbearing years slip away. He stripped me of something that should've been mine, leaving me with the pain of knowing what could have been, but never was. I thought I had felt grief before but nothing prepared me for the realization of the grief that comes with having to accept that I would not be a mother.

At this point, I had already lost so much in life. It felt like every time I took a step forward, something or someone was there to push me back. But instead of succumbing to the weight of my losses, I chose to rise. I threw myself into volunteer work, pouring my heart into helping others, something I had always found joy in. I worked tirelessly at a local food pantry, dedicating every day to giving back when I couldn't go to a typical job. This service became my lifeline, and it grew into something even more profound. I began working with local girls in my community, helping them adopt local shelters and safe houses. Together, we provided for those in need, lifting them up in ways I wished I had been uplifted when I was younger. It was this work that kept me grounded, that reminded me that even in the darkest times, there is always a way to make a difference.

Then, the pandemic hit. I was out of work, out of money, and heartbroken, watching my savings slip away. But instead of succumbing to despair, I did something I had never done before: I bet on myself. I took everything I had left—just $500—and poured it all into creating Balloonacy Boston. I knew this was my chance, my moment to rise above all the adversity I had faced, and I wasn't going to let it slip away.

Starting a business in the middle of a global pandemic wasn't just a risk—it was a defiance of everything that had tried to break me. And as my business began to grow, I encountered the same negativity I had faced as a child—only now, it was from grown women, bullying each other on social media. It felt like those playground moments had come back to haunt me. But I refused to let it take me down again.

When I was young, I made a promise to myself: if I ever had a platform, I would use it to uplift others, especially women. I would create a sisterhood, a community where women didn't tear each other down but built each other up. In my eyes, a woman in the same field as me isn't competition—she's my sister. My space would be one of love, positivity, and unwavering support. I would use my business to create that space for other women, a space that felt like the warm embrace I had known at home.

Today, my journey has shaped me into a woman who has endured more adversity than anyone should ever have to face, but it has also made me stronger, more passionate, and more determined than ever. I've learned that the road to success is never easy, but it's worth it. Every setback, every heartbreak, every loss has only fueled my determination to create something bigger than myself. It's a testament to resilience, faith, and the power of betting on yourself.

To anyone who feels like they're at the end of their rope—take a deep breath and know that it's not over. Embrace the uncertainty and take that leap of faith. I did it, and if I can rise from the ashes, so can you.

Life will try to break you. People will betray you. Doors will slam in your face. You will be overlooked, underestimated, and counted out. And when that happens, you have two choices: let it consume you or rise from it. I've had everything taken from me. My mother, my security, my dreams of motherhood. I've been knocked down more times than I can count. But every single time, I got back up. And I didn't just survive. I built something from the ashes. If you're sitting in your darkest moment, wondering how you'll make it through, trust me when I say this. You already have everything you need inside you. Bet on yourself. Take the risk. Build the life you deserve. Because no one is coming to save you, but you can save yourself!

About the Author

Dede Forgione is the magical creative mastermind behind Balloonacy Boston. Passion, creativity, and innovation are at the heart of everything she does.

Baloonacy is not your average balloon company. They specialize in luxury custom balloon decor, pushing the boundaries of design to create unforgettable experiences. Dede is often asked what sets them apart in this industry, and for her, the answer is clear: their dedication to customization, innovation, out-of-the-box thinking, and meticulous attention to detail.

Balloons are her canvas, and she has dedicated herself to transforming ordinary spaces into extraordinary experiences. Not only do they craft stunning balloon and silk floral installations, but Dede has also pioneered methods and techniques that didn't exist before, methods that have been taught and shared throughout the industry.

It is an honor for Balloonacy to be part of their clients' most cherished celebrations and a privilege to bring their visions to life, creating memories that will be treasured for a lifetime. Whether it's a grand event or an intimate baby shower, Dede thrives on the details that make each experience truly unforgettable.

At Balloonacy Boston, they don't just decorate; they create memories to last a lifetime.

www.balloonacyboston.com

Instagram: @balloonacyboston

The Power of Authenticity

Haley Fortier

The saying goes that you can't bullshit a bullshitter, which, let's face it, is the cornerstone of modern commerce. You'd think, wouldn't you, that the best way to get ahead is to be the *most* accomplished bullshitter? But no. Turns out, the real secret weapon? Authenticity. Which, honestly, is way harder. Pretending to be genuine? That takes *real* skill.

When I opened haley.henry, my first business, I wasn't just experiencing a mild case of imposter syndrome; I was practically hosting a full-blown imposter convention. I mean, really, who did I think I was? A small-town, queer kid from New Hampshire, suddenly deciding I was going to revolutionize the Boston wine scene with...natural wines and tinned fish? I spent most nights staring at the ceiling, convinced I'd accidentally wandered into some elaborate performance art piece where I was the bewildered, underqualified star.

Was I having a breakdown? Probably.

Every time I mis-stepped, which, let's be honest, was roughly every other week, I'd be seized by this exquisite dread. Not just the *oops, I forgot to water the plants* dread, but *did I accidentally sign away my constitutional rights in this lease contract* dread. Every unfamiliar spreadsheet, every cryptic wine distributor email, was a fresh opportunity for disaster. I'd lie awake at night picturing the consequences: the health inspector, a particularly judgmental Yelp reviewer, maybe even a roving gang of tinned fish enthusiasts, enraged by my sardine selection. But then, something strange happened. Months went by, and the only catastrophic twist was that I accidentally ordered a case of orange wine that tasted suspiciously like feet. And even *that* sold out. Turns out, my branded chaos was working. The monster under the bed, the one I'd been picturing wearing a tiny sommelier apron and muttering about oak aging, seemed to have taken a sabbatical. Or maybe it just decided to become a regular.

When I opened the bar in 2016, my personal ethos and vision was to promote small production wines from all over the world. Goodbye, mass-produced California cabs. So long, oaked, buttery chardonnays. I wanted to introduce people to grape varietals they'd never heard of and most likely would mispronounce for weeks. To force them to actually think about what they were drinking, instead of just mindlessly gulping down another glass of *whatever*. My previous wine director had taught me about *armchair travel* which is similar to the notion of *when in Rome*. It tells a story about where wine comes from, how it's produced, and it paints a picture of the farmer who brought it to life: the true hero at any table. And the atmosphere? This was going to be the house party you always dreamed of; the one where the rap music was just a little too loud, the furniture was vaguely worn in, and you were constantly scanning the windows for flashing blue lights. A place where you could feel both at home and slightly on the run.

Now, this is where the *authenticity* comes in because if I told you how many initial patrons didn't think that rap music was *winebar music* and people didn't think that *tinned fish* would become the shining star on the menu, I could have folded my hand, admitted defeat, and served up the kind of experience you find in a dentist office. Smooth jazz, shrimp cocktail, the gentle hum of polite boredom. But something in me, probably a stubborn streak leftover from my New Hampshire roots, kept saying, *Just keep going. They'll either get it, or they won't. And honestly, if they don't, it'll probably make for a better story later.*

Within the first three years of opening, haley.henry received multiple accolades from local, national, and global press: James Beard semifinalist, Boston's Best Awards, articles in *Food & Wine*, *Bon Appetit*, and *Wine Enthusiast* magazines. We became somewhat of a star athlete within the restaurant industry and the imposter syndrome, which had previously manifested as an internal panic began to recede. I realized, much to my surprise, that I didn't have to be a walking encyclopedia of grapes. I didn't have to conform to the norms, nor did I have to be polite, apologetic, or take bullshit emails from wine reps who asked me, "Why do you think you're qualified to have a bar?" (I don't work with them anymore). I just had to be comfortable knowing what I knew and be willing to learn more. I needed to be the person who was standing there, looking back in the mirror, that authentic self that I'm talking about. And the real turning point? The moment I knew I'd truly arrived? It wasn't the awards or the press. It was the eightysomething woman, clearly channeling her inner gangster, nodding her head to Tupac's "Gangster Party." That, my friends, is when you know you've created something truly unique. Or possibly, just slightly unhinged.

Two years later, a neighborhood developer beckoned. And because 2018 was basically a giant, simmering dumpster fire, with the #metoo movement ruling the headlines, I decided, in my infinite wisdom, that wine was the answer. Specifically, wine made by women. What better way to stick it to the man than with a carefully curated list of obscure, female-produced vintages? *nathálie wine bar* was born, a tiny beacon of estrogen in the testosterone-fueled shadow of Fenway Park. At first, it seemed like a challenging idea. A quaint, intentional wine bar amidst the sports bars and beer halls, like a tiny, well-mannered poodle at a monster truck rally. We'd be different! A refuge for the "normal" people, the ones who like to watch baseball but also secretly yearn for a glass of something that doesn't come in a plastic cup.

In our first six months of opening, *Imbibe Magazine* declared us "Wine Bar of the Year." We weren't just "the lady wine bar" in Fenway; now we were "the *award-winning* lady wine bar." #womensupportingwomen trended. I pictured tiny, digital women cheering. Cork tiaras almost happened. Suddenly, we weren't whispering about female winemakers; we were shouting. We were weird. We thrived. It was as if the women's liberation movement was back and we were leading the parade directly down Brookline Ave.

At that moment, something solidified internally for me. Something clicked. I realized that by stubbornly clinging to my vision at both bars, I'd actually created something people wanted. A community; a place where people could drink natural wine and not feel judged for their eclectic music taste. I ran our social media accounts, which looked like they had been designed by a caffeinated squirrel, and we refused to take ourselves seriously. Which, in the world of wine, is practically a revolutionary act. Turns out, people liked that.

Nine years later. Nine. That's a lot of wine. And a lot of questionable decisions. But somehow I've emerged, blinking into the sunlight, with some pride. And, dare I say, a sense of accomplishment. We've started hosting lesbian club nights at the bar so our freak flags can fly as high as possible. It feels like the right energy; Chappell Roan blaring in the background, singing about casual sex and "femininomenons." It is magnificently... us! I've somehow amassed two teams of people who, inexplicably, consider me a friend. They tolerate my playlists. They put up with my dad jokes, which, I'm told, are "endearing." They've even embraced my alter ego, Sgt. Gibbly, a personality that surfaced after a particularly long evening of gin and the nightcap of post-shift Dr. McGillicutty shots from the pub across the street. I've collected a motley crew of patrons, fellow grape juice aficionados, who are now, for better or worse, part of my extended family. We've even created friendships with our winekeys: inanimate objects to most, but respected "best friends" in our back pockets. In fact, they are such important parts of our identity as wine professionals that when one breaks, or "dies" as we like to say, we commemorate it with a full-on burial ceremony at the bar. There are currently nineteen coffins on display.

And, of course, there's my tramp stamp. A permanent relic of my youth from a time when I apparently thought I was taking life by the balls. It's a Janis Joplin quote, *Be true to yourself. It's all you have.*" Maybe I knew back in the day that this would be the mantra of my inner core. Pay no mind that the tattoo shop was in the basement of a grungy, disheveled bar room in New Hampshire. Somehow I still found clarity.

And so, I'll say it again, with the conviction of a motivational speaker: authenticity. That's the golden ticket. The secret sauce. People can smell a phony a mile away. They're like bloodhounds for insincerity. All you have to do in this life is be unapologetically... you. Don't change your flow because the tides are going the other way. Stick to your vision. Eventually, the water adjusts. Or, at least, a few slightly bewildered fish swim your way. And honestly, that's enough.

About the Author

Haley Fortier brings over 20 years of experience to the hospitality industry and is the entrepreneur of two charming, sophisticated, and energetic wine bars in the heart of Boston, Mass.: haley.henry and nathálie. Both haley.henry and nathálie wine bars are known for their carefully curated selections of natural, organic, and biodynamic wines from around the globe.

Fortier's specific vision on creating spaces in the wine world that offer inclusion, education, diversity, and undeniable vibes, has allowed her to create memorable wine-drinking experiences for seasoned oenophiles and those wanting to dip their toes into the captivating world of wine. More so, her commitment to supporting small, independent winemakers, with a focus on women-led wine operations, is what sets her apart from other wine bars in the city.

Under Fortier's leadership, haley.henry wine bar was recognized in 2019, 2020, and 2024 as a semifinalist in the James Beard Award category of "Outstanding Wine Program." She was also named in 2019 by *Food & Wine* magazine as one of the "2019 Sommeliers of the Year." Her entrepreneurial style has garnered her recognition in both local and national press, including *Imbibe*, *Food & Wine*, *Bon Appetit*, *Wine Enthusiast*, and numerous local accolades and awards.

http://www.haleyhenry.com/

http://www.nathaliebar.com/

Instagram: tin_and_gin | haleyhenrybar | nathaliewinebar

Living Your Truth

Kristin Gennetti

I came from a big traditional Italian family and was raised in Malden, Mass., just a few miles north of Boston. I grew up in a home with my mother, father, and younger brother and then my grandmother, too, in her later years. I was always surrounded by lots of cousins, aunts, uncles, grandparents, and friends. Life was always a party!

My most vivid memories were family pool parties, our city's Italian family festival, playing basketball until the streetlights went on, and playing my favorite games of Rummy 500 and Monopoly. My family described me as curious, full of energy, and wise beyond my years for a child. As a young child, I felt like an "old soul." I connected easily with adults, and I had a strong sense of empathy toward others. From an early age, helping others gave me a massive sense of fulfillment. I have seen the power in practicing one small act of kindness a day. I have learned that we truly have the power to change someone's life and what an amazing gift that is!

Throughout my childhood and adolescent years, I loved sports and school, and I always excelled academically. Going to college was never a question for me. In the 1990s, going to college was what you did after high school. People had shifted from going into the trades to venturing to college, and that was part of the American Dream, or so we thought. As I was approaching high school graduation, I applied to a few local schools, ultimately committing to Boston University where I began my college career in 1996, when I was eighteen. I arrived at Boston University and was immediately overwhelmed with the need to choose a major which in turn meant deciding on my entire life's path as an eighteen-year-old.

One day, I was flipping through a book of professions and stumbled upon occupational therapy. It captured my attention. I loved wellness and helping people, and I enjoyed being around children. This career path could incorporate all the things I love and more, so I applied to the program and was accepted. I had no idea how rigorous the science coursework would be and that I would even spend a semester dissecting human cadavers! I was making it through the coursework, studying around the clock, working two jobs (at times three jobs) and just surviving. I wasn't having fun in college, and I soon realized that these classes were not lighting a fire in my soul like I had expected them to. However, I stayed on my path because that is what you are supposed to do. I felt that time and money would have been wasted if I switched career paths, and I also did not want to disappoint my family or myself. I continued and graduated from Boston University with a class of less than fifty students, as part of one of the top programs in the country at the time. I thought, "I did it! I survived." It soon became clear that I hadn't figured out the difference between living and surviving.

In 2001, when I was ready to enter the workforce, I was hired by a public school system as an occupational therapist. I worked with children with a variety of physical, social, learning, and emotional disabilities in an elementary school. I quickly learned my role, and I adored working with children. However, as the first few years passed, I realized that there was something missing, somehow this job didn't feel like a forever thing. I didn't believe in my heart that this career was what I was called upon to do on this earth, and I felt that in my soul. I was counting down for each day to end, constantly projecting when the next vacation would come and marking red X's on calendars as the days went by. I thought, "This can't be my story. Is this it?" I decided I needed to do some soul searching and really dig deep. I knew that I was not living my truth, and I knew for sure that something was missing but what could it be?

I always had a passion for interior design, and I was a self-confessed HGTV junkie. I found myself researching home design obsessively in my spare time and daydreaming about interiors. One Sunday afternoon, after binge watching HGTV, the lightbulb went on and I decided that maybe I should get my real estate license. After all, my mom had been a real estate agent when I was kid, so real estate was in my genes! I took the real estate class in one weekend, studied, and sat for my license. I became a licensed realtor in 2004, and shortly thereafter began working part-time for a local company. I went to every single training that I possibly could to absorb as much knowledge as possible. I worked from the time I left school in the afternoon into the late evenings, every weekend, and at every single open house that I could pick up. I loved every minute of it. I met as many people as I could. I utilized my amazing mentor, who graciously dedicated so much of her time to teaching me the ropes. Soon after, my business started to grow. I felt so alive again, and I truly felt that, now, I was living my truth. For the first time in forever, I felt that I was exactly where I was supposed to be.

I found myself sitting with my clients and listening to their stories. I learned that every house and every client has its own story. Some stories were beautiful, stories of my clients building a forever dream home or needing a new home because of their growing family. However, many of my clients also were dealing with major stressors and life changes, death, divorce, and illness. I became an intimate and integral part of their lives and, on many days. a listening and unbiased ear, much like that of a therapist. My job became more than just guiding them in selling or buying a home. I was guiding them to also help alleviate as much stress as I possibly could for them while also gaining a trusting relationship with each and every one. I realized that it was a parallel to the work I was already doing as an occupational therapist. I had to identify the need or the problem and try to fix it, or at the very least, try to help.

I worked simultaneously as an OT and a realtor for seven years and hustled every day. At the time, my real estate boss encouraged me to leave my OT job to go full-time into real estate. He believed in me and thought I would go far in my real estate career. I was scared, but at the same time confident in my abilities. That same boss is my coach today, almost 20 years later. He believed in me from the very beginning. I heard a lot of noise from the people close to me when I talked about leaving my school job. They would remind me of the stability that I had, the consistent paycheck, the retirement, the benefits, and the degree that I had worked so hard to get. It was going to take something big for me to make that leap, and that is just what happened!

On August 21, 2013, at 11:19 P.M, on the night of a blue moon, I gave birth to the most beautiful blue-eyed baby girl, Milania, and my life was forever changed. I looked at my little girl with such awe and amazement. Giving life to a tiny human was God's greatest gift to me. I wanted to do better for Milania and me. I wanted to set a good example for her. I knew that it would be impossible to have two full-time jobs and be a mom, and I could not leave my beautiful baby every day to pursue a career that was not my soul's purpose. My time away from her needed to be well spent. Milania's pure existence gave me the courage to pursue what set my soul on fire. I owed it to her and I owed it to *myself* to be the best possible version of myself that I could. I decided to leave my OT career at the school and go full-time into real estate. Six days after Milania was born, I was out showing homes! I felt like a burden had been lifted. I had made a decision to live my truth for me and for her. This was a defining moment and a major catalyst in my life.

As the years passed, I was building my clientele and my sales, and I had the flexibility to be home with Milania and watch her grow. The lightbulb went on again and I decided that I wanted to grow my business in my hometown of Malden and be a trusted resource to its residents. I wanted to open a boutique office and really establish myself. In 2019, I did just that. I opened a small boutique office in the heart of the developing Malden Center. I knew that the future for Malden was bright. Malden Center was going to be redeveloped and be booming with new restaurants and businesses. I found a chic office space and a broker to believe in my vision.

We created a modern, warm, and inviting space for agents and clients. Within the same year, we got off the ground and cut the ribbon at our grand opening, the pandemic hit, and the office was shut down. We quickly pivoted to selling real estate from our homes and on Zoom calls, while home-schooling our children. My friends in business were calling each other for advice and support, and I wanted to be a voice of positivity and strength. I decided to create a business group called the Malden Business Connection. I connected with business owners on a weekly call, and we supported each other through the pandemic and beyond. We shared business ideas and provided moral support to one another during an unprecedented time. The bonds that were formed during that time were amazing! My skill set as an occupational therapist shined through. In 2020, through patience and perseverance, amid chaos and uncertainty, I had my best sales year in real estate.

I have grown our presence in Malden and become Malden's trusted and number one realtor for the last six years. I have a wonderful team of agents that I am grateful to work with. Although we serve clients all over Massachusetts, as well as some nearing states, I feel most proud to be part of Malden's "come up." I always believed in Malden, and I am grateful that the people of Malden have believed in me. I will never forget where I came from, and that is very important to me. I am proud of the many awards and accolades I received along the way, but my biggest accomplishment in life has truly been raising a strong, fierce, kind-hearted and resilient little girl. Milania is now eleven years old and loves school and sports, and in particular, hockey. She is an old soul, wise beyond her years and she reminds me so much of myself at that age. Milania has been able to witness me building a business while raising her. I hope that through my example she will see that women can shatter all the glass ceilings, and we can do absolutely anything we put our mind to.

At forty-six years young, I am just a girl from Malden with a lot of hustle and heart, who is living, not just surviving. I will help lift as many people as I can until the wheels fall off! I hope to make a crater-sized impact on the world and hope that I inspire you to do the same. Live your truth for yourself and for those around you. Share your story when you can and inspire others. (Thank you for the inspiration J.B., it came when I needed it the most!) Dream big, extend grace, never withhold your gifts from the world, and always remember that love is greater than fear.

About the Author

Kristin Gennetti brings over twenty years of experience in real estate in and around Greater Boston and the North Shore, serving as both a buyer's and seller's agent. A high-touch realtor known for her extensive market knowledge and her unmatched devotion to clients, Kristin's success is based almost exclusively on positive referrals and repeat clients. She earns the respect of her clients by working tirelessly on their behalf and by always offering them her candid and honest advice.

Kristin was recognized as the number one agent in Malden, per MLS, for six consecutive years and was ranked number five statewide in volume by Century 21 in 2024. Kristin was awarded the AREAA (Asian American Real Estate Association of America) A-list award as a top producer in 2024. She was also recognized in 2024 among the top fifty Massachusetts real estate agents on social media as well as the best dressed by *Boston Agent Magazine*.

Kristin leads Century 21 North East | The Kristin Gennetti Group, overseeing a team of eleven realtors in a boutique office in the heart of downtown Malden. A self-motivated leader, Kristin is also a second generation realtor. Kristin is a multi-million-dollar, award- winning producer in the industry and is coached by the number one real estate coaching company in the country. Kristin prides herself on her commitment to her clients and constantly elevating her skills. Kristin truly loves her work, and her many glowing reviews tell a story of two decades of both her hustle and her heart.

www.kristingennetti.com

Facebook: @kristingennettigroup

X: @kristingennetti

Instagram: @kristingennettirealtor or @thekristingennettigroup

https://www.linkedin.com/in/.kristingennettiaylward

Sprinkled with Purpose: A Recipe for Growth, Community, and a Cake Decorating Movement

Jelissa Lamboy

This chapter is dedicated to my beautiful bright girls, Alessia and Ahlani, and my beloved grandmother, Vavó Eduarda Cabral.

Growing up, I was lucky enough to always know what I was passionate about. Baking excited me from the time I was a little girl. Whether it was a coloring book, a toy, or a game, I always gravitated toward anything related to sweet treats. Some of my favorite childhood memories include decorating cookie kits with my mom and brother, baking with my Nana Marilyn—who taught me how to follow recipes—and serving as the ultimate taste tester for my Vavó's dishes and elaborate desserts.

I'm the proud daughter of an immigrant mother who came to the United States from Portugal with my grandparents in 1979, carrying dreams of a better life. My grandparents worked tirelessly to provide their children with more opportunities, creating a legacy of resilience and success for future generations. My grandfather, a local legend, has dedicated over twenty-seven years to janitorial work at Boston University. His sacrifices, along with my Vavó's, have given me the opportunities I have today. From battling and beating cancer to showing up every day for BU's students, his strength and dedication inspire me, and I am honored to be part of his legacy.

I am also a proud Puerto Rican woman who deeply cherishes my roots. My heart is forever connected to the island, and I dream of moving one day to immerse myself in my family's history and culture. I am a first-generation college graduate, a self-made businesswoman, and, most importantly, a mother to two incredible little girls!

Raised by a single mother who had me at a young age, I watched her work multiple jobs while still being my support system as a child. Though we faced struggles, she always ensured I had everything I needed, no matter the sacrifices she had to make. We moved between multiple cities and schools, which often left me feeling like an outsider. But through all the changes, one thing remained constant—baking. It became my escape, my safe space, and my home.

As a little girl, I was shy and quiet, preferring to keep to myself. My quietness also made me an easy target, so I grew up feeling extremely self-conscious and out of place. I struggled with anxiety long before I even knew there was a word for it. For years, I questioned where I belonged. That changed when I learned about a vocational school offering a culinary arts program. My mom worked tirelessly to save and find our first permanent home so I could attend. Determined to secure my spot, I wrote a three-page essay advocating for my acceptance. When I received my acceptance letter, I was ecstatic!

Over the next four years, I trained under an incredible teacher and immersed myself in the culinary world. At sixteen, I landed my first job at a local bakery—conveniently located right across the street from my house. Working in the industry gave me invaluable hands-on experience, and it solidified my love for baking even more.

When it came time for college, my number one choice was Johnson & Wales University. It was an absolute dream—not only was I accepted early and the first in my class, but I was also later awarded the Presidential Scholarship. I was beyond excited to start this new chapter. Up until then, my life had been pretty sheltered. My mom was extremely strict—so much so that I didn't stop having a bedtime until I moved out for school! College was my first real taste of freedom. I could make my own decisions, meet new people, and explore life on my own terms. It was a huge adjustment.

My freshman year, I had a work-study job in the school dining hall, surviving on $7.25 an hour while recovering from surgery. By sophomore year, I landed a job at a local bakery in Rhode Island and proudly attended my graduation for my associate degree in baking and pastry arts.

Then came junior year—when everything became overwhelming. I was trying to maintain my spot on the dean's list, plan for my future career, manage a long-distance relationship, study every free second, and budget just to pay my bills. My schedule was stretched impossibly thin, and eventually, the pressure caught up to me. At one point, I was juggling three part-time jobs: nannying, working as a baker/barista four days a week, and cleaning halfway houses and group homes for a private cleaning company. I barely had any time for myself. I was opening credit cards without understanding the long-term consequences, struggling to afford food because tuition was so high, and constantly dealing with car issues and unexpected life expenses. On top of that, I was battling crippling anxiety and had no idea how to ask for help.

As a young adult facing some of my hardest and most trying times, I had no choice but to figure things out on my own. There were days I had to choose between groceries, gas, or rent. At one point, I couldn't even afford my textbooks, so I'd spend all night at the university library photocopying pages to keep up with my assignments and essays. At the same time, I was in a long-term, emotionally abusive relationship, which I had been in since I was sixteen. My self-worth was at an all-time low, and my judgment was clouded. The weight of life became unbearable. Eventually, I couldn't bring myself to show up for my classes. Most days, I stayed in bed, calling out of work, not eating, and ignoring my friends. I was lucky if I had the motivation to respond to a single text.

The responsibilities felt too heavy to bear, and balancing it all seemed impossible. After speaking with the university counselor, I made the incredibly difficult decision to take a medical withdrawal for my mental health. The guilt was crushing. I was halfway through my junior year, so close to finishing, and I felt like I had failed myself. The fear of judgment and shame consumed me, and I spiraled into one of the darkest periods of depression I had ever experienced.

I moved back home, but it wasn't long before I found myself living out of my car. At just nineteen, I was still trying to navigate life, but my mom's expectations felt overwhelming and out of reach. After experiencing a taste of independence, returning to a home filled with strict rules and limitations was suffocating. I suddenly had limited say in most of my decisions, and the adjustment felt impossible. My mom, as tough-loving as she is, has always been an extremist when it came to discipline. She believed in turning struggles into lessons, and because of that, I learned to survive by figuring things out on my own. No matter how impossible a situation seemed, I always found a way. Eventually, I decided it would be easier to be on my own. I couch-hopped between friends' houses, unsure of where I truly belonged. Those next few months were rough. My passion felt distant, and the support I desperately needed wasn't there. I started waitressing to make ends meet, but that lifestyle led me down a path I wasn't proud of—drinking too much, making poor decisions, surrounding myself with inauthentic people, and eventually, isolating myself completely.

Luckily, with the support of my best friend, who has always been there to lift me up during my darkest moments, I was given the opportunity to move in with her family. I'll forever be grateful to her—she has always been the one to help me rediscover my light.

Now, fast forward to 2017: I'm newly single, focusing on my health, setting boundaries, and I land a lead role for the pastry team at Fenway. Hands down, this was one of the coolest and most memorable experiences of my career. Humble brag, but I had the chance to design cupcakes for The Pedro Martinez Foundation Gala. I created fun, unique flavors, and the next day, the executive chef pulled me aside to tell me that Pedro himself had complimented my work!

The adrenaline of working there was insane. Depending on the Red Sox schedule, I'd work shifts from five a.m. to one p.m., then go home, only to return for an overnight shift at six p.m. I was such a sprinkle maniac that I would go home and BAKE in between shifts instead of sleeping—because I was just so inspired and excited. This job will always be one of my favorites to reminisce about.

Eventually, though, I made the tough decision to move on, feeling that there wasn't much room for advancement in that role. But man, do I miss waking up at four a.m. and seeing the sunrise over the field at Fenway. Don't worry—I took WAY too many pictures and Snapchats to make sure I never forgot those moments (dog filter included—if you know, you know).

That summer, I started a new job as an assistant pastry chef at a popular steakhouse. At twenty-one, I had dedicated the year to focusing on myself and figuring out this new chapter as a young adult. On my very first day, one of the chefs introduced himself, and there was an undeniable connection between us. Before we knew it, we had fallen in love, moved in together, and within that same year, we had our beautiful daughter. Things moved unexpectedly and quickly, but our little girl became the best thing that ever happened to us.

Financially, we faced a tough decision: I had to return to work when she was just a month old. It was a new challenge—balancing the role of a new mother while pumping in a dry storage room, keeping up with dessert production, and still being a team player. All the while, I felt like I was missing out on so many milestone moments with my baby. My mental health began to decline again, so we made the decision for me to stay home while my partner picked up late night shifts. The next few months were tough, as all the financial burdens fell on my boyfriend. Managing parenthood, lack of sleep, and navigating new responsibilities while trying to find time for each other was harder than we ever imagined. But we worked at it every day, and I'm so grateful we did.

In 2019, I applied for a position as the head pastry chef at a new restaurant being built. The chef who interviewed me turned out to be the best boss I've ever had in the entire industry. He believed in me before I even fully believed in myself. He gave me the space to be truly creative and allowed me to express myself fully through my desserts. But beyond that, he shattered all the stereotypical barriers I had come to know in the industry. For the first time, I worked under a chef who saw me as an equal in the kitchen, who respected me as an individual, and who made the workplace fun instead of intimidating. He offered so much grace when life responsibilities got in the way—whether it was my kids being sick or when I was going through personal challenges. The trust he instilled in me, as well as the accommodations he made to better fit my life, will forever leave me endlessly grateful. Within my first year as pastry chef, I was entrusted to run the entire pastry department on my own. I got to create mini pastries for weddings, corporate events, and special occasions. I also had the honor of creating plated desserts that were later featured in *Northshore Magazine*, *Phantom Gourmet*, and *The Boston Globe*. I even had my own feature article with *OCTOCOG*.

Out of the thirteen years I've spent working in kitchens, this was the first where I truly felt safe as a woman. The environment he created for our entire team was unlike anything I had ever experienced, and I'm truly blessed to have worked in such an amazing restaurant. He gave me a safe place to do what I love most, and even when I made the transition to running this business, he was incredibly supportive. To this day, he continues to cheer me on. I owe so much to Ben Lightbody for motivating me to be brave enough to take the leaps I have, and I'm forever thankful for the entire team at Grove, who continue to treat me like family and offer me a second home there.

When COVID hit, like so many others, I lost my job. At the time, I was pregnant with my second daughter, and my boyfriend—also a chef—was unemployed as well. The fear and uncertainty were overwhelming. But as all great women do, I decided to adapt, evolve, and take a giant chance on myself. With limited options and many restrictions, I started baking out of my apartment. It was a wild idea in the middle of a global pandemic, but at that point, I felt like I had nothing to lose. One late night, I sat up brainstorming names, and that's when it came to me—The Sugar Connection. I wanted to merge my love of desserts with the heart of what I truly cared about: connection. I designed a logo, created branding stickers, and launched a holiday menu for Christmas. To my amazement, I received over thirty orders—some from people I didn't even know. That was thirty people who believed in me. For the next year, I built fun holiday menus, poured my heart into my baking, and began growing my brand. Then, unexpectedly, my grandmother passed away.

This was the hardest loss of my entire life. My grandmother was my inspiration, my biggest cheerleader, and the most powerful, unconditional love I had ever known. She always saw the best in me and supported every decision I made. I remember when I entered an online baking competition where votes determined your ranking. People could also pay for extra votes. When I tell you this woman was determined to keep me on top—she spent hundreds of dollars a day, checking out faster than I had ever seen her buy anything on QVC at two a.m. There was no stopping her when it came to me. She was my lifeline, my purpose. Losing her was the most tragic and traumatic experience I've ever faced.

I ultimately decided to take a break from baking. I was unmotivated, depressed, and isolated. Months went by, and my daughter—the one who had inspired me to start my business—was about to turn one. Devastated that my grandmother would miss such a special moment, I went to bed praying to her, and that night, she visited me in a dream. She didn't speak, but her presence was so illuminating. It felt like a sign—a temporary healing for my grief. The next morning, I knew I had to honor her in some way. She had always told me that when she passed, she would visit me as a blue butterfly. So, I booked a smash cake photoshoot for my daughter and baked her a cake—the first one I had made in months. I decorated it with bright blue butterflies, edible gold, and sugar pearls. And just like that, my spark was reignited. I truly believe she pushed me to try again, and to this day, I feel her encouragement in everything I do.

As I finish writing this chapter in a coffee shop, "Make You Feel My Love" is playing overhead, and it just so happens to be her birthday. I know it's her sending a sign, and also probably her stalking me like she always joked she would. I just know for sure she's guiding me, pushing me to keep going every day. Also yes, I am currently sobbing in a café full of people, but it's fine... we're fine. I'm just grateful to continue to feel her embrace and influence as I take more leaps in this business and in life!

Now that I finally felt ready to start baking for my business again, orders were coming in slowly. I was hard on myself for taking the break I did because I knew it had created a disconnect with my clientele. I even considered a complete career change when, one day, I saw on Instagram that a local candle shop was hosting candle-making classes and looking for a business to collaborate with. Around that same time, I had attended a paint night and thought how cool it would be to incorporate art with cakes. This seemed like the perfect opportunity to give the concept a try.

After rescheduling multiple times out of fear of failure, I finally partnered with Vivian, and in July of 2023, we hosted our very first cake and candle class. The response was incredible— my social media was flooded with messages asking when the next class would be. That's when I decided to lean into the demand and trust the process. I spent the next few weeks reaching out to local small businesses, breweries, and restaurants to partner with. What started as a small class of sixteen quickly grew into a class of forty, with over fifty sold-out events and dates.

As my oldest daughter was about to enter kindergarten, I also decided to homeschool her. I followed through for the entire year, balancing the role of teacher, while caring for my then three-year-old, managing the business, and, of course, keeping up with household responsibilities. As you can imagine, it became overwhelming. I wasn't fully prepared for just how demanding everything would be. I found myself handling sales, marketing, social media, production, content creation, advertising, website development, design, media, photography— the list seemed never-ending. Thankfully, I've had amazing friends who have helped me set up and break down these events so I could focus more on these other major parts. A special thank you to my soul sisters, Jo, Caitlin, Mandy, Ciara, and of course, my partner, Francois, who has been a major supporter. Even my daughters play a part, helping clean the turntables, making cute favors for the guests, and being my mini taste testers for new recipes.

Although there's a lot on my plate to curate these events, it has also given me a new sense of identity—one that's separate from motherhood. It allows me to reconnect with myself and align my passion for baking with my love for connecting with people. I'm home most days of the week, with the exception of these classes, so in many ways, they provide me with an escape to be social again and take a much-needed break. It's been such an honor to meet so many incredible people, and it's made this business feel even more rewarding. I've had guests tell me how an event helped distract them while they were freshly grieving a loved one. I've had a group of girls use the class to celebrate a friend who courageously left an abusive relationship. I've had a woman and her sisters come for her first night out since giving birth. We've cried together, laughed together, and shared so many amazing memories.

I'm endlessly grateful for the relationships I've built with such beautiful humans. Every class, I leave with new friendships, and I hope to continue sharing that experience with everyone who joins. I even have group chats to stay in touch, and I often receive random life check-ins that are so heartwarming. I've had guests come alone, meet new people, exchange numbers, and some even go out together to dine after the class. Since meeting new people can sometimes feel intimidating, I'm so grateful that my workshops help encourage making new friends. People from as far as Connecticut, New York, and Rhode Island have traveled just to be a part of these experiences. It truly feels like a dream for strangers to believe in me, see my vision, and support it. The privilege of facilitating new relationships and creating a space where people feel welcome and accepted is truly a gift.

As I reflect, I see just how much I've grown, even as imposter syndrome tries to creep in. Despite life's challenges, my commitment to spreading joy and fostering meaningful connections has never wavered. A big part of this mission is collaborating with small, family-owned restaurants, where we host our classes to help bring exposure to their businesses and highlight their unique menus. Seeing them thrive and knowing we play a small role in their success is incredibly rewarding. We've collaborated with incredible small businesses like Top Mix, Ciao, Rose Bar, and Publico and have worked with schools to offer cake decorating classes that encourage kids to explore their creativity. We've also designed custom cake decorating kits for individuals with developmental disabilities, giving them a fun and expressive way to create edible art.

Beyond that, we've partnered with major brands like Sugar Factory, Harpoon, Sam Adams, The Royal Sonesta, and Omni Hotel in Boston. We've co-hosted team-building events for corporate companies and special gatherings for women's social groups. The most fulfilling part of this journey is hearing from guests who share how our classes have impacted them— providing a safe space to express themselves, connect with others, and feel truly heard. Sharing my passion for baking and human connection isn't just a business; it's a privilege. Our goal is simple: to make life sweeter, one class at a time. We create a welcoming, inclusive space where people can embrace the moment, step outside their comfort zones, and try something new. Community is at the heart of everything we do, and we're grateful for the opportunity to meet new people, build connections, and create lasting friendships.

I truly believe I'm here for a reason, and the power of this business reaches people because of what it represents— connection. That's the foundation of our name and mission. Food is a universal language, a love that transcends location, language, and differences. It brings people together to share laughter, create memories, and find comfort in moments of happiness, sadness, or grief. This business is about more than just desserts; it's about amplifying the love I pour into everything I create and becoming part of life's most cherished milestones. When families look back at photos of their first birthdays, weddings, or baby showers, and see the cakes and dessert displays I created, I feel deeply honored to have played even a small role in those moments. The ability to spread love through my desserts is a gift, and I hope to continue sharing that message with the community.

I'm incredibly proud to be the first Latina-owned cake decorating event business in Boston and the pioneer of pop-up cake decorating classes in the state. Along this journey, we've been fortunate to be featured on WBZ, CBS, The Hub Today, and 7NEWS Boston. Our work has been highlighted in articles such as "Top Five Culinary Classes to Take in Boston" in *Boston Uncovered*, "The Ultimate Winter Bucket List" in *Meet Boston*, a cover feature in *MassLive*, and "10 Women-Owned Businesses Worth Knowing in the Boston Area." Since 2023, we've been voted one of the top three bakeries in Haverhill and even featured on the Bold Like Her podcast.

Giving back is also at the heart of what we do. We've had the privilege of contributing to fundraising efforts by partnering with incredible organizations such as the Make-A-Wish Foundation for Massachusetts and Rhode Island, Miss America and Miss Teen USA, The Boston Marathon, and Mass General Hospital in support of their pediatric cancer care, emergency response team, and Home Base veterans program. I also recently launched Sweet Escape, a monthly giveaway designed to support those struggling with mental health by offering a free class. Whether someone is dealing with stress or anxiety or simply needs a moment of peace, this experience provides a chance to step away, reset, and create something beautiful. As a mother and someone who personally battles anxiety and depression, I know how overwhelming life can feel—balancing family, career, self-care, friendships, and personal growth isn't easy. That's why I created this giveaway: to offer a safe, welcoming space where someone in need can take a breath, reconnect with themselves, and find relief through creativity. We all deserve a moment to pause, heal, and express ourselves, and I want to help make that possible.

If you'd like to nominate yourself or someone you love for Sweet Escape, please send an email to thesugarconnectionbakeshop@gmail.com.

Each month, a new winner is selected to join a class and experience the joy of decorating in a supportive, fun environment. I truly believe that creativity has the power to heal, uplift, and bring people together. This business has saved me in ways I never expected—it gave me purpose, identity, and a deeper connection to my community. None of this would be possible without the incredible support from all of you! Cake decorating is more than just frosting and sprinkles—it's a form of self-expression, a way to find peace, and an opportunity to create something meaningful.

Overall, I am incredibly proud of the business I've built, knowing that this is just the beginning. The flexibility of balancing my role as a part-time stay-at-home mom while hosting events has given me a newfound sense of purpose. Raising my two bright, loving daughters while showing them firsthand that it's possible to pursue my dreams and do it all is truly a gift. After two C-sections, overcoming mental health struggles, self-isolation, healing from past traumas, financial hardships, years of therapy, and pushing through every obstacle, this business—and my children—are my greatest accomplishments. And while we are still just a pop-up, I have complete faith that we will continue to grow, succeed, and eventually build our own brick-and-mortar space to create even more lasting memories for those who support us.

Thank you for allowing me the space to be vulnerable and share my journey. My greatest hope is that my story inspires you to pursue your own dreams and success. You are better off giving your dreams everything you've got rather than letting life pass you by, wondering, "What if?" because you hold the key to your deepest desires. In moments of doubt, challenge yourself. Prove to anyone who has ever questioned your abilities that you are capable of anything. And most importantly, remind yourself that simply existing and striving to be better already makes you powerful! We are all worthy of greatness. You possess infinite potential. What makes you unique is what makes you shine. You are the magic!! And if it ever feels too hard, if you ever doubt what you're capable of, know that my door is always open—to be your biggest cheerleader, a listening ear, and a new friend.

Stay Sweet and Sprinkle Kindness,

Jelissa Lamboy

About the Author

Jelissa Lamboy is a Latina entrepreneur, pastry chef, and the visionary behind The Sugar Connection, Boston's first Latina-owned pop-up cake decorating event business. With a lifelong passion for baking and a deep love for community, she has transformed her craft into an interactive experience, bringing people together through creativity, self-expression, and, of course, cake.

Her journey wasn't always easy. From working multiple jobs to navigating financial hardships, mental health struggles, and personal challenges, Jelissa has overcome adversity with resilience and determination. She studied baking and pastry arts at Johnson & Wales University and honed her skills as a lead pastry chef at some of Boston's top establishments, including Fenway Park. But during the pandemic—while pregnant with her second daughter and facing job loss—she took a leap of faith, launching her business from her apartment.

Since then, The Sugar Connection has grown into a thriving movement, hosting over fifty sold-out events across Massachusetts in collaboration with local restaurants, breweries, and major brands like Sugar Factory, Sam Adams, and The Boston Omni Hotel. Her mission is simple: to make life sweeter, one class at a time, providing a welcoming space for people to connect, create, and step outside their comfort zones.

Jelissa is also passionate about giving back, working with schools, community programs, and organizations like Make-A-Wish and Mass General Hospital. Through her business, she continues to inspire, uplift, and sprinkle purpose into everything she does.

Instagram: @thesugarconnectionbakeshop

TikTok: @thesugarconnection

www.thesugarconnectionbakeshop.com

From Passion to Following Your Heart, and Making It Your Profession

Natalie Lelless-Mochi

If you had told me years ago that I would build a career enhancing people's beauty and confidence, working alongside some of Hollywood's top talent, becoming a crucial part of a bride's special day, and transforming women's self-perceptions and self-worth, I would have laughed. But life has a way of leading you exactly where you're meant to be. Looking back, I now see how every challenge, every risk, and every lesson guided me to this moment.

Makeup has always been a part of my life. As a child, I was captivated by its transformative power—how a swipe of lipstick could make someone feel confident, how a touch of shimmer could light up a face. It wasn't just about the makeup itself; it was about how it made people feel. I saw firsthand how it changed self-perceptions, helping people carry themselves with more confidence.

Growing up in a small town, I struggled with self-esteem. My curves, once a source of teasing, were suddenly embraced as I got older. This back-and-forth shaped how I saw myself. Makeup became my refuge, not as a way to hide, but to enhance. When I had to get thick glasses as a child, I hated how they made me look. I would sneak my mom's and babcia's makeup any chance I got because it made me feel prettier. Once I was old enough, I experimented with application, color, and technique (long before YouTube tutorials even existed).

My love for makeup grew when we moved to a new town in sixth grade. My neighbor, who worked for Lancôme, became my first beauty mentor. She did my makeup for dances and proms, and in return, I became the go-to artist for my friends. Looking back, I was already running my own little makeup business before I even knew what entrepreneurship was. Call me a mini Estée Lauder!

At the time, though, I didn't see makeup as a career. My parents, a schoolteacher and a businessman, emphasized education and stability. In the '80s and '90s, makeup artistry wasn't considered a real profession unless you were in Hollywood (spoiler: I eventually got there!). No one around me saw it as a viable path, so I never considered it either. Instead, I set out to become an FBI profiler, thinking that was my dream. But what I didn't realize was that true success would come from following my heart, not just a predetermined plan.

While studying in Washington, D.C., and interning with the FBI, I was introduced to the world of luxury beauty. Watching other girls use high-end products sparked my curiosity. I wanted to understand the difference and experience it for myself. I remember asking my mom for $15 to buy a M.A.C Lipglass, and she couldn't understand why I wouldn't just get a drugstore one. But for me, it wasn't about the price; it was about the feeling.

To afford the products I loved and learn more, I got a job at M.A.C. doing lips and, later, worked at Victoria's Secret Beauty during the holidays. Looking back, makeup was always calling me, I just hadn't realized it yet.

Later I moved to Florida and found myself at a crossroads. Should I pursue a career in law or continue my dream of FBI profiling? I was working at a small law firm when I first moved there, but I had no clear direction. So, like any 20-something figuring out life, I threw myself into bodybuilding. To afford training, I paid my trainer with makeup services for her photoshoots and competitions. At 22, my work was published in *Oxygen Magazine* (a huge milestone I didn't even recognize at the time). Social media was in its infancy, MySpace was the main platform, and I wasn't thinking about career-building. Yet, no matter how much I ignored it, makeup artistry kept finding me.

A few years later, I moved to Chicago, and everything changed. I still remember the day Smashbox Cosmetics opened its flagship store on Michigan Avenue—it was a star-studded event. Jennifer Aniston was in town filming *The Break-Up* and happened to be shopping there. When I saw her looking at products, I instinctively grabbed a brush to help. What I didn't realize was that the general manager for Smashbox Midwest and the two founding owners were watching.

They handed me their card, took my information, and a few weeks later, I got a call: They wanted me to train at their studios in L.A. I laughed and declined at first. But as fate would have it, I eventually found myself on a plane to Los Angeles.

At Smashbox Studios, I trained with top artists like Lori Taylor Davis and Scott Barnes, working with Hollywood elites, from Jennifer Garner to the Kardashians. But I quickly learned that building a name in the industry takes time. To support myself, I leaned into another skill: managing people's lives. Through my contacts, I became an executive assistant to some of the biggest names in business, a role that sharpened my business acumen and, unknowingly, prepared me to run my own makeup empire.

After a few years, I moved back to Boston. My first solo wedding makeup job for a close family friend reignited something in me. That moment made one thing clear: I was ready to build my own makeup career.

For years, I balanced my work as an executive assistant while growing my makeup business. I worked over sixty-hour weeks, dedicating nights and weekends to weddings, red carpets, photo shoots, and building a loyal clientele. I focused on perfecting my craft, hired a coach, and dove into mindset work.

In 2017, my corporate job unexpectedly ended, pushing me to stop investing in things that no longer aligned with my passion. By 2019, I was running a six-figure makeup business while still working as an EA. I had won awards, been published in magazines, and gained recognition, but I still wasn't fully betting on myself.

Eventually, I did.

I noticed a gap in the bridal industry. Too many brides were rushed or given generic looks, and products didn't last. I wanted to change that, so I reimagined my services, focusing on creating a luxury experience from start to finish: personalized consultations, long-lasting applications, and premium touch-up kits tailored to each bride.

My goal was simple: I wanted every client to feel like the most radiant, confident, and empowered version of themselves, whether it was their wedding day, a red carpet event, or a photoshoot.

Raising my standards came with its own set of challenges. Some questioned my pricing, compared my services to others, or hesitated to invest. But I worked with coaches and an energy healer to overcome my own limiting beliefs, evolve, and grow into the person I am today. This personal growth helped me stand firm in my values. When clients book me, they're not just paying for makeup—they're investing in confidence, peace of mind, and an unforgettable experience. That's the kind of impact I've always wanted to make: creating a space where every woman feels empowered and like the best version of herself.

In 2025, I began mentoring other beauty professionals to help them develop their mindset for success. After years of working with coaches and healers, I felt it was time to pass on the lessons I had learned. My goal is to empower others to realize they can create the life they dream of, just as I have.

But my mission extends beyond my clients. I want to inspire other artists and entrepreneurs to break free from molds, charge what they're worth, and build businesses aligned with their unique vision. Pay attention to the subtle signs that guide you toward your passion. Makeup artistry was always calling me, even if it took me a little longer to answer. Following your heart will always lead you to your highest potential.

Living a life of many twists and turns is part of the journey—it's not the final chapter. True success comes from breaking free of limiting beliefs, healing from past wounds, and letting go of the need to please others. Trying to meet someone else's expectations will only hold you back. Authenticity is the key. When you stop comparing yourself to others, you open the door to your own unique path forward.

Most importantly, remember that time isn't linear. Success doesn't follow a strict timeline, nor is there a rule that says you must reach milestones by a certain age. You're on your own journey, moving at your own pace. Don't let anyone rush you off the path before you've reached your destination.

Being featured in *Slaying the USA: Slaying Boston* is an honor. Boston has shaped me, challenged me, and given me the opportunity to build my dream career. But my story is about more than just me. It's about every client I've worked with, every artist inspired by my work, and everyone I've helped discover their own beauty and confidence.

If there's one thing I want people to take away from my journey, it's this: You don't need permission to create the life you want. Success isn't about following the crowd: it's about knowing your worth, staying true to your passion, and following your heart. The magic begins when you believe in yourself

About the Author

From following her heart to building a multi-six-figure beauty business, Natalie has become a leading name in luxury beauty. With over twenty-one years of experience, she is known for creating flawless, camera-ready looks that enhance natural beauty while lasting through high-definition photography and long wear.

Her expertise has been trusted by Hollywood celebrities like Jennifer Garner and Kim Kardashian and reality stars from *The Real Housewives* to *The Bachelor*, and she has been featured in *Style Magazine*, *Vanity Fair*, *InStyle*, *People*, *Bustle*, *Brides*, *Boston Magazine*, *Fox News*, *CBS*, and more. Her artistry graces runways, branding campaigns, and high-profile events.

Specializing in luxury bridal and editorial makeup, Natalie offers an elevated experience with custom lip colors, expert touch-ups, and a seamless process that ensures her clients feel radiant from the first look to the last dance. She also works with entrepreneurs, executives, and public figures, helping them exude confidence in branding shoots, media appearances, and corporate events.

Beyond makeup, Natalie mentors fellow artists, helping them shift their mindsets, overcome limiting beliefs, and realize their beauty business goals. More than just artistry, her work is about empowerment, helping women worldwide see their worth, embrace their power, follow their hearts and become their most confident selves.

Whether perfecting a bride's wedding glam, preparing a celebrity for the red carpet, or coaching beauty professionals, Natalie's mission is clear: to empower, elevate, and transform.

http://instagram.com/beauty.bynatalie_

www.natalielellessbeauty.com

37-Year-Old Libra Female is Seeking Harmony and Inner-Balance

Lianne Leventhal

This story is dedicated to my daughter, Elle, who already has a keen eye for fashion and design, and like her mother, is a force in her own right. To my sons, Simon and Dean, who remind me to pause and find joy in the simple things—like endless giggles and silliness. And to my husband, Alex, who never once told me my dreams were out of reach and picked up some of the slack at

home—like handling bedtime routines so I could steal a few
more hours of uninterrupted work.

As an entrepreneur, mother, wife, community leader, and champion of several causes, I've started to ask myself: Is it possible to have it all? Maybe it's my balance-seeking Libra nature whispering in my ear, always nudging me toward harmony—within myself, my work, my family, and the world.

I've always been self-driven. Growing up in a desirable, New York suburb with highly educated, hardworking parents, I was the embodiment of the American Dream. The resources were there; the expectations were high. I felt an immense responsibility to make the most of it—not just for myself, but for something greater. That drive would serve as both a catalyst and a curse.

Like many first-generation kids with ambitious parents, my career options were narrowed down to two: doctor (like my father and grandfather) or lawyer. Given that I nearly broke out in hives at the sight of a math equation or the mere thought of chemistry class, medicine was ruled out. Law seemed like the logical next step. I was creative, imaginative, and a fairly good writer—arguing my case in a courtroom had a certain dramatic appeal.

So, law it was... for a while.

Then came freshman year of college and the occasional binge-watching of classics like *Sex and the City*, *The Devil Wears Prada*, *How to Lose a Guy in 10 Days*, just to name a few. Naturally, I found myself captivated by the sharp, determined, impossibly well-dressed, and completely unrealistic journalists in these films. Andrea Sachs, running through Manhattan in her Chanel boots while tackling impossible deadlines? Andie Anderson, cleverly weaving her way through a seemingly superficial assignment to expose a deeper truth. There is, of course, Carrie Bradshaw, who idealizes the role of being a journalist in New York by living a glamorous, cosmopolitan lifestyle filled with fashion, romance, and cultural experiences—I wanted that. A career in journalism—one where I could write about extensive topics, wear great shoes, and be taken seriously—felt like my true calling. As Jackie Kennedy famously once said, *"Being a journalist seemed the ideal of both having a job and experiencing the world, especially for anyone with a sense of adventure."* Yes, please. So I pursued a double major in journalism and political science, determined to carve out a space in the media world. During college, I landed a coveted summer internship at a subscription-based business magazine catering to C-suite executives and board members of publicly traded companies. It was serious. It was respected. It was exactly what I needed to confirm that I was, indeed, on the right track. I started with fact-checking, then quickly moved on to research and writing, eventually scoring my first published byline.

Then, 2009 happened.

The recession hit like a wrecking ball, obliterating job prospects for my peers and me in nearly every industry. Media was in crisis. Magazines and newspapers were hemorrhaging money, laying off staff left and right. What next? I had to get creative. As I reflected on my passions, my fondness for fashion and design had always been present. Those closest to me would say that the evidence was always there. Home videos of my toddler self, show me blissfully unwrapping new outfits, immediately putting them on, and twirling around in front of my family. I always had an eye for style, a natural sense of what worked, and enough outside validation over the years to confirm it wasn't just in my head. (I was named "Boston's Best Dressed" in *Boston Common Magazine*'s September 2024 issue).

Then, an opportunity presented itself: a luxury women's eveningwear designer needed a writer to create content for their website, catalogs, and editorial collaborations. It was writing, it was fashion—two of my passions colliding. Before long, I was running my own department as public relations director within the fashion house.

One day, I was writing product descriptions; the next, I was securing placements in *Cosmopolitan*, *Glamour*, and *Marie Claire*. I worked directly with celebrity stylists, making sure A-listers were perfectly dressed for the red carpet. I spearheaded a major celebrity endorsement deal and campaign. I was casting models, overseeing photoshoots, taking red-eye flights to LA during awards season. The job was fast-paced, demanding, and glamorous—but, like any high-pressure industry, it was also exhausting and often underappreciated.

Amidst the whirlwind of fashion and PR, I met a guy from Boston. He was debonair and compassionate. The long-distance routine quickly became our norm—late-night Amtrak rides, early-morning shuttle flights, alternating weekends between cities. Eventually, he made the move to Manhattan full-time. Two years in, we got engaged. Three years in, we got married. Four years in... we were saying goodbye to New York.

Where to? Boston, of course.

The move was a major life change—one I didn't fully grasp at the time. Let's face it... Boston isn't exactly known for its fashion sensibility. Nor does it come remotely close to rivaling New York as the media capital of the world. Deep down, I knew a real career in fashion wouldn't be possible there. Let's also note that I was four months pregnant when I uprooted to Boston.

On top of everything, my father had already been sick for a couple of years, and soon, I would find myself kissing his forehead for the very last time. I was 33 weeks pregnant with my daughter, his first grandchild, when my father passed. I was shattered. But for the sake of my unborn baby, I knew I had to push forward and be strong.

The following year was a whirlwind. We moved into a new condo, and I became deeply involved in its gut, renovation, and design. Every meeting with our design team fascinated me. The way they mapped out a perfect floor plan within minutes of walking into a space, how they layered fabric, furnishings, and finishes—it was like watching a Monet masterpiece come to life.

Each detail was deliberate, yet nothing felt rigid. That was the moment my love for interior design and architecture was born.

At the time, my daughter had just turned one, and I was very much living in my husband's world. Born and bred in Boston, his family had deep roots in the city spanning three generations. Meanwhile, I missed my own family and friends back in New York. My new friendships consisted mostly of my husband's friends and their significant others. I needed more. I needed to rediscover my identity—this time, as a wife, mother, and aspiring interior designer.

So, I enrolled in an interior architecture program, studying everything from foundational design principles to the evolution of architecture. I learned to balance school while being a wife and mother—until life threw me another surprise. I got pregnant again. And then, two years later, pregnant once more.

Fast forward to 2020–2021—the COVID era. Everyone's social calendar had vanished, and I was at home trying to keep it all together with two toddlers and an infant. Before COVID, I had immersed myself in nonprofit work, serving on the boards of the Boston Ballet and Boston Children's Museum. My husband was also involved in several boards and ran his own company within the family business, so our lives were constantly in motion. But the lockdown forced me to slow down and reflect on what I truly wanted.

It was during this time that I met my now best friend—purely by chance. She, too, had recently moved back to Boston from Manhattan and was an interior designer who had worked for reputable firms before launching her own. We quickly bonded over our shared love of design. She was experienced, knowledgeable, and encouraging. I confided in her that I had never worked for a design firm and, with three young children, working full-time for someone else wasn't realistic. "Great taste and an eye for design are three-quarters of the battle," she reassured me. "Sometimes that's even more important than professional experience."

With a great cheerleader in my corner, I took a leap of faith. I started my own company, tackling small projects in my own home, then for friends, then for my husband's company. Before long, I had a working portfolio.

Now, as I reflect on everything I've built and continue to accomplish, I feel an overwhelming sense of pride and purpose. As a mother, wife, sister, daughter, friend, business owner, designer, and community leader, I refuse to be confined to just one role. I could have easily existed in someone else's shadow, but my ambition and self-driven nature wouldn't allow it. Instead of merely existing, I am living.

Call me foolish and naive, but I believe we, women, can have it all. If we manifest it and aren't afraid to take chances—and most importantly, lift and support one another—then anything is possible. I've learned that no matter what city I live in, I have the power to carve out my own identity and purpose.

About the Author

Lianne Leventhal is a Boston-based interior designer and the founder of Beyond the Common, a full-service firm that primarily specializes in high-end residential interiors. Her work has been featured in *Boston Magazine,* as well as interior design publications. She is a mother, wife, and active member of her community. Lianne serves on the board of trustees at Boston Children's Museum and was formerly a board advisor at Boston Ballet for ten years. Lianne is an art enthusiast with a fine appreciation for contemporary art and can be found traveling to national and international fairs.

She has received accolades for her style and fashion sensibility and was named "Boston's Best Dressed" in *Boston Common Magazine.* Currently, she resides in the Boston area with her husband, three young children, and her Cavalier King Charles Spaniel Lady Penelope. Lianne is perfectly happy sitting in her self-designed English garden, drinking tea, and daydreaming.

https://www.beyondthecommon.com
Instagram: @beyondthecommon

Defining Moments

Dr. Naomi Goldman

Our defining moments are not the ones where everything falls neatly into place. They're the ones where all the shit hits the fan.

It was 2020. The world had just shut down. As a 33-year-old associate dentist, I suddenly found myself completely out of work for three months, with zero income. I had a seven-month-old baby, was pregnant with my second child, and, in the midst of it all, my parents announced their separation. They also told me they would be selling the practice—either to me or to someone else.

Let me back up for a second. I feel I have to put this into context for you- this practice was my home. I had been working in this office since I was fourteen years old. I worked my way up from stamping envelopes to running the entire front desk and was there every summer until the time I became a dentist. I knew the patients, I worked alongside all the employees, and in 2014 when I finally got my DMD degree and finished a one-year residency, I jumped right in and started practicing alongside my father. By 2020 I had already been working in the practice for six years and had just started to get a feel for managing a team. And there was no way I was giving that up.

While I had always envisioned myself owning the practice, the timing certainly wasn't ideal. Looking back, I should have been terrified. I was about to take on a million-dollar loan in an uncertain economy and would be going on maternity leave just two weeks after purchasing the practice—once again with zero income.

But I wasn't scared. *I was excited.* This was my opportunity to shape something of my own, to build and grow a business that aligned with my vision. And I had my husband on my side—an extremely business-minded person who is always there to bounce ideas off of, to remind me of my wins, and to celebrate my success.

I've always had a strong belief in myself, a knowing that I would just "figure it out"—whatever that "it" may be. I believe in my ability to see a problem and find a solution, or to seek out those that have a solution I don't know about. I think that's really important in entrepreneurship, maybe the most important quality. If you want others to believe in you, you must first believe in yourself.

My vision was simple: create a practice with a spa-like feel that emphasized patient education, oral wellness, and high-end treatments and technology. I knew this vision would carry us forward into growth, but also unite us in building something better, something beautiful. Unfortunately, with that vision came some huge risks, and I had to somehow prove that I wasn't going to lead my team over a cliff.

I had the vision, but now I had to empower the team. Leadership wasn't something that was intuitive to me. As a naturally shy, non-confrontational person, I really struggled with balancing my need to people please with the knowledge that I had to create structure and boundaries to allow my employees to thrive.

At first it was all wrong. I overcompensated, trying to gain respect from older employees who had previously been co-workers, and I led with strict policies and little flexibility. I quickly learned that this was neither effective nor enjoyable for anyone. Instead of earning me respect—it was alienating me from my team.

So, I changed. I became the kind of leader I would want to follow--someone who treated employees like family, who cared about their personal lives, and who understood that work-life balance wasn't just a buzzword but a necessity. And just like that, the team turned around.

Now that I had a team that would follow me, the next step was giving them a stake in the game. The first major change I implemented was a team-based bonus system. I believed that if my team had a vested interest in the practice's growth, we would all thrive together. I couldn't ask them to work harder, to go the extra mile for patients, if there was nothing in it for them. More importantly, I knew that a happy, motivated team would create an unparalleled patient experience. Patients don't just remember good dental work—they remember how they were treated, how they felt in the chair, how the team made them feel seen and heard.

In order to achieve my vision I had to make one very crucial decision: whether to stay in-network with insurance companies. Reimbursements to dentists from insurance companies were shrinking every year, and costs continued to increase. I saw two possible futures: either we became a high-volume, factory-style practice with rushed appointments, or we transitioned into a boutique, out-of-network practice focused on oral wellness, cosmetics, and high-quality care.

While staying in-network obviously didn't support my vision, going out-of-network meant potentially losing a massive portion of our patients and essentially rebuilding the practice from scratch.

I had ten employees depending on me for their livelihood and I had a family to support. The stakes were high, and not everyone was on board with my decision. Some employees left, but I knew in my gut it was the right decision. I knew it with every fiber of my being. I just had to be strategic about how we implemented the changes so we could mitigate the damage.

The key was to retain as many existing patients as possible while attracting new patients who valued the type of dentistry I wanted to offer. My first question was, "How do I create the kind of patient loyalty where people stay, even when they have to pay more?" The answer: provide an experience so exceptional that cost becomes secondary.

Beyond restructuring the business, I saw a growing demand for a spa-like dental experience. Dental anxiety is incredibly common, and at the same time, there's a rising demand for cosmetic enhancements. I recognized an opportunity to blend the two—creating a space where patients felt relaxed and pampered while also receiving cutting-edge cosmetic treatments.

I envisioned an environment where patients would not associate their dental visits with stress or discomfort but instead with self-care and rejuvenation. From the moment they walked through the doors, I wanted them to feel at ease—greeted by calming aesthetics, soothing scents, and a hospitality-driven experience that felt more like a luxury spa than a sterile medical office. I introduced amenities such as neck pillows, noise-canceling headphones, weighted blankets, and personalized treatment plans tailored to both oral health and aesthetic goals.

Beyond just comfort, I focused on treatments that catered to the modern patient—someone who values both conservative care and excellence. The days of aggressive, invasive procedures are fading, with more people seeking subtle, natural-looking enhancements that preserve their teeth while enhancing their smile. I invested in state-of-the-art technology to provide minimally invasive options like no-prep veneers, digital smile design, laser dentistry, and high-end whitening treatments that deliver remarkable results with little to no downtime.

Additionally, I trained my team to approach patient care with a hospitality mindset—ensuring every visit felt personal, unhurried, and customized to the patient's unique concerns. We shifted the focus from simply treating dental problems to proactively helping patients achieve the smile they always wanted—whether that meant addressing small imperfections, offering preventive treatments, or designing a long-term aesthetic transformation.

Marketing became another crucial area of transformation. Traditional advertising—Google ads, magazine placements, and sponsorships—brought in virtually no new patients. Even Facebook ads proved less effective than I had hoped. But Instagram? That changed everything. I realized that before I could ask people to become patients, I had to provide them with value first. I started sharing educational content, simple tips, and information about non-invasive treatments that people didn't even know existed but were actively seeking out. I also shared before and after photos of my work, because seeing is believing. By positioning myself as an authority in the area of general and cosmetic dentistry, I saw an influx of patients who were coming to me for a second option or for cosmetic treatments, even though they already had a general dentist who may have been doing those treatments but just wasn't taking about it.

Finally, I invested in technology that empowered my patients. For years, I had felt like a car mechanic trying to explain why someone needed a new engine—how did they know if I was telling the truth? They couldn't see what I saw, and without visual proof, it was easy to feel skeptical or even dismissive of a diagnosis. That realization shifted my entire approach to patient education. I knew that if I could bridge that gap—if I could give patients the ability to see their own dental conditions the way I did—it would transform not only their understanding but also their confidence in making informed decisions about their care.

So, I brought in high-quality imaging and diagnostic tools that allowed patients to take an active role in their treatment planning. Digital scanners became an essential part of every visit, allowing me to show patients exactly what I was seeing— whether it was a cracked filling, early signs of enamel erosion, or plaque buildup in hard-to-reach areas. These scanners also replaced outdated, uncomfortable impression techniques, giving patients a clearer picture of their dental health while eliminating the mess of traditional molds.

I noticed an immediate change in how patients responded. Instead of simply nodding along as I explained their treatment needs, they started asking deeper questions. They became more engaged, more proactive about their oral health, and, most importantly, more trusting. The skepticism that often surrounds dental recommendations faded when they could see the problem for themselves. And with that trust came an openness to preventive treatments, to long-term planning, and to the kind of high-quality care that ultimately saved them from more invasive procedures down the line.

Looking back, I'm always shocked by how much our team has accomplished over the past three years. Through leadership growth, bold business decisions, and a commitment to innovation, I've built a practice that reflects my core values: integrity, education, and a relentless pursuit of excellence.

For all of this, I have my parents to thank, for instilling in me the confidence to dream big, the resilience to chase those dreams, and the wisdom to recognize opportunity when it knocked. For entrusting me with their practice—a gold mine of potential just waiting to be unearthed—and to my husband for standing by my side, unwavering, through every challenge and triumph. My family's belief in me has been my greatest advantage, and for that, I am endlessly grateful.

About the Author

Dr. Naomi Levy Goldman was born and raised in Peabody, Mass.—the very town where she now practices.

As the daughter of a dentist and a dental hygienist who built and ran a practice together, she grew up immersed in the world of dentistry. As a teenager, she took an interest in the craft of dentistry and the art of running a business while working by her parents' side.

Dr. Goldman attended the University of Connecticut for both her undergraduate and dental degrees before completing a one-year residency at the VA in Augusta, Maine. In 2014, she joined her parents' practice, bringing with her a deep commitment to patient care and an emerging interest in cosmetic dentistry. While still in dental school, she discovered her passion for enhancing smiles and pursued extensive continuing education in the art of veneers.

Owning the practice was always part of her vision, but she never anticipated how much she would come to love the business side of dentistry. In 2020, she officially took over the practice, embracing both the clinical and entrepreneurial aspects of the profession.

Today, Dr. Goldman is bringing her vision to life—creating a spa-like dental experience that prioritizes oral wellness, patient education, and exceptional care. With a focus on comfort and service, she continues to blend artistry and expertise, helping patients achieve healthy, confident smiles.

@dr.naomigoldman

www.levygoldmandentistry.com

Be(a) the Change.

Bea Murphy

At an early age, I knew I wanted would be an entrepreneur; I just didn't know exactly where I would land. I thought I would take over the family business, maybe open my own boutique shop, but little did I know it would be far from either of those visions. Growing up with immigrant parents from Romania, I knew what hard work and grit looked like. My parents moved from Romania in the 1970s, landed in South Boston, ventured down to Braintree, and finally settled in Weymouth, on the South Shore. My father owned his own jewelry store in downtown Boston from 1975 until 2022 (or thereabouts because, let's be real, do entrepreneurs ever retire?), and I grew up helping my dad in his store my entire life. I saw what it took to run your own business and have carried those lessons with me.

My mom was the opposite—she didn't have a traditional job but focused on raising me and my brother. I witnessed the hardships of running your own business as well as the toll it can take on family life. One could say, I am the perfect combination of both my parents: a hardworking entrepreneur and a nurturing mother.

My competitive nature showed up early. I started on dance teams at a young age before my focus shifted to a love of sports. I was introduced to field hockey in the fifth grade and fell in love. I played throughout high school at Thayer Academy and college at Bentley University, even winning the NCAA National Championship with my team during my sophomore year. Being part of a team taught me so much, and that sense of teamwork has deeply shaped my work ethic.

After graduating college, I had no real idea what I wanted to do, as most kids do. I earned a marketing degree with a management minor from Bentley, but what did that really mean for my future? I took the first job that came my way, which was working for a company that sold copy and fax machines in downtown Boston. Not only did I have to wear a suit every day to work, but I also had to cold call, knock on doors, and convince people to buy copy machines from me. After three months of doing this and earning "rookie" of the quarter, I quickly realized that selling copy machines wasn't for me.

I moved on to work for a fashion house, Akris, in Boston on the wholesale side—and I loved it! What wasn't to love? I worked on Newbury Street, surrounded by beautiful clothing, models, designers, and so much creativity. This opportunity eventually led me to New York City, where I spent two years continuing my work for Akris on Madison Avenue. But, like so many Bostonians, I knew there was only one Boston, and the pull of being closer to my family and friends eventually brought me back to the Bean.

This was the beginning of what I consider the true "retail" era of my career. I worked for Staples Corporate, Lyn Evans for Potpourri Designs, and eventually landed at Rue La La in South Boston as an associate buyer. On paper, it was every fashion lover's dream, but the reality of endless grinding and struggle led me to leave the retail industry behind. During my time at Rue La La, I married my husband Brian in 2012 and had my two children, Reilly in 2014 and Maddie in 2016. Those years were tough. I was leaving the house at five a.m. to catch the train while my mom watched my kids, and I wasn't getting home until six p.m., feeling like I was failing at both work and motherhood. My kids were miserable. I was miserable. Something had to change.

Then came one of those "aha" moments. I realized I needed a career change—something with more flexibility, something that would allow me to pick the kids up from school, take them to sports, and just *be there* for them. After poring over Excel spreadsheets to figure out budgets and plans, I decided to take the leap. I found a brokerage that felt like home and valued family life as much as I did: Lamacchia Realty. In 2017 with my son then three years old and my daughter one year old, I started as a brand-new agent with no prior real estate experience and quickly became a force on the South Shore. In those early years, I almost doubled my business year over year, and now I average fifty to sixty deals annually. Best of all, I've been able to be the mom I always dreamed of being.

I've realized there's no true work-life balance; it's all a blend. I might be up early catching up on emails or writing offers from the sidelines of my kids' games, but I never miss the important moments—concerts, games, you name it. My career change allowed me to do both: succeed professionally and prioritize my family.

Even while thriving as a realtor, I've always felt a desire to do more—to contribute to something bigger. In 2019, I lost my college best friend to cancer at just thirty-eight years old. To honor her memory, I dedicated my time to riding in the PMC (Pan-Mass Challenge), an annual bike ride that raises billions for Dana-Farber Cancer Institute. Then, in August 2022, my son was diagnosed with type 1 diabetes—a challenge that took my family by surprise. Adjusting to this "new normal" of carrying medical supplies everywhere and always having snacks on hand, I realized that this was my new cause. I've since dedicated my time to fundraising for type 1 diabetes, even launching an annual hockey fundraiser that I hope to grow bigger every year.

From being the first generation to graduate college in my family, to running my own successful business, to being a mom of two, at the end of the day I know what inspires me and drives my inner voice, which is to be the change. Whether I am helping a first time home buyer win their first home, helping sellers downsizing from the home they raised their family in, or being a mom and raising two respectful kids, I love helping others and making an impact in my direct world, and others. I live my life with no regrets, and one day when all that's left is this book and two grown Murphy kids, I want people to remember Bea Murphy, as the woman who made a change, even if it was a small one.

About the Author

Bea Murphy is a true native to the South Shore, born and raised in Weymouth where her parents still reside. She was a retail buyer for about twelve years, with a two-year residency in New York City. Having experienced the endless grind and burnout of retail buying, along with the burden of travel, Bea knew it was time for a change after the birth of her second child. She wanted something that allowed her more control over her time where she could not only be phenomenal at her job, but also be the mother she wanted to be. In 2017, Bea dove headfirst into real estate, and her only regret is not doing it sooner. Year after year, Bea continued to grow her business and continues to sell over fifty homes a year. Bea has also dedicated herself to fundraising for two very important causes that are dear to her: Dana Farber Center and type 1 diabetes research. In 2019, Bea lost her best friend of over twenty years to cancer, and in 2022

Bea's son was diagnosed with type 1 diabetes. She has been called Super Woman, the Energizer Bunny, and the woman who can get anything done, and the minute you meet her, you'll understand why.

www.beamurphy.com

Instagram: Bmurphy388

Beyond the Numbers: A Journey Deeper Than Your Bank Account

Jenae Murphy

October 27, 2013, changed me. Waking up with an unshakable pull to check on my nana, I didn't know I was about to step into a new chapter of my life—one shaped by loss, love, and transformation. She had been the heart of my life, the foundation of every warm memory, and the only stable home I had ever known as a child.

When I opened the door, I felt it before I even saw it: She's not here. The room felt different—emptier. Her soul had moved on, and I stood there, numb, trying to grasp the weight of what that meant. How do you put into words that the person who taught you unconditional love, despite a language barrier, was gone? How do you tell the people who love her just as much about the harsh reality?

I was the one who had to break the news to my family, but at that moment, I could barely comprehend it myself. It felt impossible, unreal. Yet, as painful as that day was, it was also the beginning of something I couldn't yet see—a journey of healing, self-discovery, and purpose.

Losing her shifted everything. It made me look at life, love, and legacy in a new way. It planted the seeds for who I was becoming—the person I am today.

For years, one of my responsibilities as a child was filling out my nana's money orders. I can still picture it—carefully writing out the details, making sure everything was correct, especially the one for the life insurance company. It was a routine, something I did every month without question. Along with that came reading her bank book—watching what came in, what went out.

So, when the time came to lay her to rest, I couldn't understand... *Why wasn't there any money to bury my grandmother?*

I was lost. Confused. The only person who knew the answer was gone. I turned to my mother, searching for clarity, but that was a dead end. It felt like an unspoken tradition—money wasn't something we talked about, not even when it mattered most. And yet, here we were, struggling to give Nana the proper farewell she deserved.

I had no control, no say over what happened next. Instead, someone who wasn't even around was making the decisions about the woman who raised me. It felt unfair, unsettling—like standing on the outside of something that should have belonged to me. I felt uncomfortable and awkward.

That moment planted a seed—one I wouldn't fully understand until later. The way money was handled, or rather, not handled, had consequences. And I never wanted to feel this powerless again.

Here I was, standing at a crossroads with my two daughters, trying to find my financial footing while still carrying the weight of my grandmother's passing. The confusion and uncertainty didn't end with her funeral—it followed me, wrapping itself around every decision I had to make. I felt like I was drifting from one painful situation to another, barely keeping my head above water.

On top of that, I was dealing with someone close to me who had a mental illness no one knew about. The chaos, the unpredictability, it drained me. But then, a realization hit me like a wave: I didn't have to stay in this situation. I had something powerful on my side—choice.

And I chose *me*.

For the sake of my kids, for the sake of my peace, I made the hardest but most necessary decision: I shut the door. Not just physically, but emotionally, mentally, and spiritually. Once that choice was made, something shifted inside me. I started to find myself again. The fog of confusion began to lift, and for the first time in a long time, I felt a sense of clarity.

That moment wasn't just about leaving, it was about stepping into my power. And from there, my journey truly began.

By 2019, life felt aligned. I was working with mentally ill adults, my kids were thriving in extracurriculars, and I was on track to earn my bachelor's in human services—one step closer to becoming a therapist.

"Dream job... here I come!"

Then, 2020 changed everything. Plans unraveled, certainty vanished, and I was forced to rethink everything.

I met my then-boyfriend, a nineteen-year veteran in the financial industry, and one day, I happened to overhear one of his meetings. Then, I heard the magic words:

"You won't ever lose money."

I was shocked, doubtful, and intrigued all at once. Could this really be true? If so, why hadn't I heard it back in 2013 when I needed it most?

I had to know more—and if it was real, I had to tell everyone.

I listened intently until his meeting ended, and then the lightbulb went on. I had to ask, "Why can't I do what you do?" He hesitated, warning me that this business required constant interaction with people. As someone who didn't naturally strike up conversations, doubt crept in. But my passion for sharing this knowledge overpowered any fear. When COVID-19 forced me to leave my job, I took it as a sign—my entrepreneurial journey had begun.

My financial situation took a hard hit, and I was struggling. I remember crying endlessly, completely broke, with no clue what to do next. All I had was faith, and I clung to it. Somehow, I made it through and officially got licensed before the fall of 2020. I threw myself into training, studying those who had built successful careers in this industry. But I also saw the ugly side—greed, arrogance, and deception.

I knew I had to do things differently. My path had to align with my morals and values. I refused to take away someone's choice or mislead them because, to me, this was a matter of life and death. Money conversations shouldn't feel overwhelming or unsafe. People deserve understanding, clarity, and ease when discussing something as crucial as their financial future. So, I created that space.

Everything came full circle from 2013 to now. I had to reflect, dive into neuroscience, explore meditation, and truly understand the power of the mind in shaping reality. Before I could help others, I had to first understand myself—especially my own relationship with money. That journey of self-discovery led me to create the transformative spaces mentioned in my bio.

A wise friend once told me, *"Once you change your seat, you change your perspective."* That stuck with me. So many people stay in the same seat, ride after ride, never realizing that a shift in perspective could transform their entire financial journey. That's why I'm here—to encourage that seat change. Because you deserve it. We all do.

About the Author

Jenae Murphy is a visionary entrepreneur, financial educator, and the founder of Financial Therapy LLC, a company dedicated to helping individuals and families understand their relationship with money. With a deep passion for financial wellness, Jenae specializes in addressing financial trauma, shifting money mindsets, and providing strategic pathways to generational wealth.

Through her innovative programs, including the series "If Money Were a Person" and six-week Financial Therapy Healing Camp, Jenae integrates financial literacy with emotional resilience. She believes that true financial stability is not just about numbers—it's about understanding personal money habits, overcoming limiting beliefs, and creating sustainable wealth-building strategies.

Jenae's expertise extends to young adults through tailored financial education programs designed to make complex financial concepts accessible and engaging. Her mission is to bridge the gap between financial knowledge and emotional well-being, ensuring that individuals at all stages of life feel empowered to take control of their financial future.

In addition to her coaching and educational programs, Jenae hosts the podcast Seamless Money Secrets where she interviews entrepreneurs, thought leaders, and financial experts, shedding light on financial behaviors, success strategies, and wealth-building mindsets. As she builds a multi-million-dollar platform, Jenae continues to expand her reach, making financial therapy an essential tool for long-term financial success.

With a commitment to transforming lives, Jenae Murphy is redefining what it means to have a healthy relationship with money, one conversation at a time.

www.financialtherapyllc.com

Instagram: @jenaesfinancialtherapy

Redheaded and Relentless: A Story of Growth, Grit, and Giving Back

Stacy Murphy

I grew up a redheaded, freckle-faced, scrappy kid—raised by my dad and brother. Ours wasn't a traditional household; it was chaotic, but we knew my dad deeply loved us. I learned early how to be tough, independent, and resourceful. I didn't grow up dreaming about building a photography business or making a difference through service—I was trying to keep up, navigate life, and figure out who I was in the world.

But that unconventional beginning shaped everything. It taught me to follow my curiosity, say *yes* to experiences, and show up with heart—even when I didn't have it all figured out. Borrowing a camera in high school immediately sparked joy. Photography became a way to connect, give back, and tell stories.

My life hasn't exactly followed a straight line. Four years of college took me eight—because life happened. There was a year in Hawaii, a backpacking trip through Europe, and plenty of detours. But I always kept going. I raised three incredible kids, built a business I love, and poured my energy into causes that matter.

Through it all, I've tried to live with heart.

Living Loud, Living Real

At my core, I want a real life that's big-hearted and full of adventure. That spirit has taken me all over the world. I've lived in a van in Iceland, traveled across Ireland, Italy, France, Germany, Russia, Amsterdam, England, Greece, the Netherlands, and Switzerland, and explored many corners of the United States. I've skydived, scuba-dived with whale sharks at the Atlanta Aquarium, and—yes—even dived with sharks. My friends call me the queen of hobbies and certifications. I'm a certified yoga instructor and a birth and postpartum doula. I've taken cooking, sewing, resin art, and kitesurfing classes. I have run the Boston Marathon three times. I am endlessly curious and never done learning. My dream is to invent something. *Shark Tank*, here I come.

But no matter where I travel, Boston has always been home. It's where I raised my family, built my photography studio, and where I continue to serve my community. My dad loved Southie—he thought it was the greatest place on Earth. So, I'm a little proud that my daughters chose to stay in Boston after college. It feels like we've come full circle. I hope my son returns to Boston after he graduates from college. My husband and I love dinners in the North End and enjoy everything Boston offers.

More than a Lens

I started my photography career shooting sports—fast, intense, and all about timing. But after having kids, everything changed. I wanted to slow down, be present, and capture the real, everyday moments that mattered. That shift led me to open my studio in Walpole, focusing on photographing women, especially during pregnancy and motherhood.

More than twenty years later, my work is about more than just photos. It's about helping women see themselves again. I didn't plan for any of this—it just unfolded, and I kept saying *yes*. But my most meaningful work hasn't always been in the studio. It's been in service. I've always felt a deep pull to honor those who've given so much. I serve on the Walpole Veterans Committee, helping organize events throughout the year to honor our local heroes. If I can be a role model to youth— to teach them that showing up for veterans counts—I'll consider that a life well-lived.

A few years ago, I volunteered with Honor Flight New England, a nonprofit that takes veterans to Washington, D.C., to see the monuments built in their honor. I was paired with a Korean War veteran, and we spent the day together—he was being celebrated for his service, and I was quietly in awe. Watching him take in those monuments with tearful reverence was humbling. It reminded me why we show up, why we remember.

Not long after, I was asked to take portraits of seventeen veterans heading on another Honor Flight. That experience inspired a deeply personal photography project, 90 and Beyond, where I offer complimentary portraits to anyone over ninety. I've had the honor of photographing a gentleman on his hundredth birthday and a couple who survived the Holocaust. After their session, they came to my home for dinner, and my family sat and listened for hours as they shared stories of survival. It was one of the most profound evenings of my life. It's an honor for me to spend time with men and women who have lived such inspiring lives.

Legacy through Portraits

One of the projects closest to my heart is my *40 Over 40* series. It began with a simple question: What if we celebrated women over forty in a way that made them feel beautiful and worthy—just as they are?

Because here's the truth: I've heard too many women say, "I'll do a session after I lose weight," or "I'm too busy," or "I'm not photogenic." Trust me, I've said all those things too. But what we're really saying is, "I don't feel worthy of being seen." And that breaks my heart.

Society has a way of whispering that aging makes us less visible and less valuable. I want to change that perspective. We deserve to be seen. We deserve proof that our lives matter.

I lost my mother to suicide when I was eight years old. That tragedy shaped my life in unimaginable ways. It was tough, but it taught me resilience, empathy, and the passion to live every day to the fullest. After she passed, we realized there were no photos of her—she didn't like being photographed. She thought she was overweight. She didn't feel beautiful.

Having no images of her fuels my mission.

I don't just want women to have "pretty" pictures, either; my goal is for every woman to leave a love letter—in the form of a portrait—to someone they love.

Some of the women I photograph are nervous. Some haven't been in front of a camera in years. But something magical happens during those sessions. We discuss motherhood, marriage, divorce, careers, grief, second chances, and dreams. I'm not just taking photos—I'm documenting. By the end, I'm not just their photographer.

I'm their friend.

The *40 Over 40* project inspired my podcast, *Living Your Best Life: The Midlife Edition.* I sit down with women I've photographed to talk about life—the highs, the heartbreaks, the hilarity of it all. We've lived, we've learned, and we're still showing up. That deserves to be heard.

So to the woman reading this, wondering if her life is enough, let me say this: Your life is the epic story. You don't have to be loud to matter. You have to be kind. You have to show up. Give what you can. Love the people around you. That's the real impact.

Being included in *Slaying Boston* means a lot to me. It's not about recognition—it's about representing the everyday work of showing up, giving back, and staying true to who you are. I'm proud to stand alongside other women making a difference in their own way, and I'm grateful to be part of a community that values strength, heart, and purpose. Boston is full of strong women doing remarkable things. I'm honored to stand among them.

I'm not done exploring. I'm not done learning. And I am definitely not done living.

To my husband Donnell, thank you for being my rock, standing beside me, and always cheering me.

Saylor, Emery, and Grady—remember, you are the authors of your own story. Write pages that will be worth reading. You are my reason for living a life that matters. I love you.

To my brother and my friends, I wouldn't be where I am today without all of you—to my Elephant Tribe, having you all as friends is worth more than any worldly possession. I mean that with all my heart!

About the Author

Stacy Murphy is a portrait photographer and content creator based in Walpole, Mass. With over twenty years of experience helping women feel confident and beautiful in front of a camera, Stacy specializes in maternity, motherhood, and women's portrait photography. Her mission is simple: to ensure every woman leaves her studio feeling celebrated. Her heart-driven project, *90 and Beyond*, offers complimentary portraits to anyone over ninety.

Beyond photography, Stacy is deeply committed to giving back. As an active member of the Walpole Veterans Committee, she helps organize community events to honor and support local veterans. Through her work with Honor Flight New England, she accompanied a Korean War veteran to the national monuments in Washington, D.C.—a journey she describes as unforgettable. She's recently become a mentor with Big Brothers Big Sisters of Boston, bringing full-circle a quote from her high school yearbook: *"To make a difference in a child's life."*

Stacy is an adventurer at heart, with a severe case of wanderlust. She always has a suitcase full of camera gear, including a drone, underwater housing, and various gimbals. She recently returned from Saint John, where she documented a weeklong retreat as a content creator, capturing moments in both photo and video. From scuba diving to kitesurfing, her hobbies are as adventurous as her spirit, and she dreams of exploring the world's oceans through underwater photography.

At the heart of it all, Stacy is a proud mom to two daughters, Saylor and Emery, and a son, Grady. Donnell, her husband of twenty-six years, is her best friend. They have renewed their vows every five years to celebrate their life and love together; they share a love of travel, adventure, and creating meaningful memories. Whether she's behind the lens, giving back to her community, diving into new experiences, or simply soaking up time with family and friends, Stacy lives with intention—making every moment count and striving to leave a positive mark wherever she goes.

For more information or to view her portfolio, visit her website for women's portraits at www.stacymurphyphoto.com or her website for newborn and maternity portraits at www.stacymurphyphotography.com.

Instagram: @stacymurphyphoto

LinkedIn: https://www.linkedin.com/in/stacy-murphy-a20366274/

Facebook: https://www.facebook.com/stacymurphyphotography/

And So She Speaks

Sarah Noelsaint

Have you ever felt like your life had no purpose? Like you saw no end, no light, no future—just a constant feeling of being lost?

I did.

For years, I questioned why I was here. Every day, I wrestled with the weight of existence, searching for meaning in what felt like an empty void. Until one day, I picked up the pen and decided to rewrite my story. And suddenly—after years of darkness—there was light. For the first time, I felt purpose.

I see my life in two parts: walking in darkness, unsure of what my purpose was—before I found my self-worth and true purpose—and after.

When I reflect on the turning point in my life, I think of the moment I finally realized my worth. The moment I decided to love myself unconditionally. The moment I refused to let the opinions of others define who I was. I fell in love with social media and content creation because they allowed me to tell stories—stories that could bring us all together.

Ever since I was a little girl, I've had the desire to create—to express myself and make others feel seen. Maybe because, for so long, I felt invisible, unheard, and misunderstood. I remember watching *Annie* and being captivated by how she overcame everything life threw at her. The way she inspired me—I wanted to do that for others. I wanted people to feel seen the way she made me feel seen.

But life had its own plans.

I was bullied, made to hate the way I looked. And after something so sacred—something meant for marriage—was stolen from me, I felt like my voice was silenced for years. The one time I said "no," I was still silenced.

So I created.

It was the only way I knew how to express myself. I made videos, bringing ideas to life. I sang songs that said everything I didn't know how to say. Throughout high school, that creative spark was my safe space. Just create—that was the only thing that brought me peace.

After high school, I had a choice. Follow my dream of creating, or take the more "rational" path: nursing... every Haitian parent's dream. And I know they were only guiding me with what they knew—what they believed would give me security and a better future. They thought they were helping me choose what was best. But it wasn't mine. My heart screamed *create*, while the voices around me whispered, *"Be logical, you're never going to make it, that kind of dream is a 50/50 shot.*

I felt like I was being pulled in two directions—what I truly wanted, and what would fulfill the dreams my parents had for me. Eventually, I convinced myself that their dream was mine, too. But I knew deep down it wasn't. Even in nursing school, even in the clinicals, even in the scrubs—I felt the tug. That part of me that still wanted to create never left.

And even after graduating, working as a nurse, and getting through school a second time, that feeling didn't go away. Nursing gave me something—I could connect with people, help them, love them, and inspire them. But it still didn't fill me completely.

Then I moved into my first apartment with my now-fiancé. I sat on my bed, looking around at everything I had—an amazing partner, a steady job, a beautiful space. I should've felt full. But I didn't. There was still a void. That same quiet knocking at my heart that had always been there. I sat there crying, feeling like I was on a little boat in the middle of the ocean. I could go anywhere I wanted... but I had no idea where to go.

A few weeks later, after an argument, that old feeling came back—not as heavy as before, but familiar. The feeling of letting someone else's opinion determine how I saw myself. I turned to my little sister and said, "I think I need to start loving myself. I mean, really loving myself." She looked at me and said, "Yes. All your life you've taken care of others. Take care of you."

That changed everything.

I made a promise to say *yes* to everything I had been too afraid to do. That promise turned into a fitness journey, where my focus became loving myself into the strongest version of me. Then I got my first tattoo—"Exist Loudly"—permanently inked on my skin. It was my first true act of self-love. A declaration to myself: *I will not shrink. I will not hide. I will exist loudly, unapologetically, and in my truth.*

Then I started a podcast with a friend, and while we were waiting to record one of our episodes, I felt this warmth and peace wash over me. This quiet joy. I remember sitting there thinking, *I want to create.* The ability to take something from my head and bring it to life—it gave me purpose again.

I left my full-time nursing job for something new, hoping that change would spark something. But I got fired. And weirdly, I was okay with it. Something in me said, *Maybe this is the opportunity you were praying for.*

That's when I decided.

I wasn't going back. I didn't know exactly what I was going to do, but I knew I wanted to create and inspire. So I did. Terrified, unsure, but hopeful, I bought a desktop and a vlogging camera. My fiancé encouraged me, reminding me that if this was truly my passion, I owed it to myself to try. His support gave me the final push I needed.

For the first time, I was choosing what made me happy, what brought me fulfillment.

At the time, I thought the hardest part was taking the leap.

I was wrong.

One of the hardest things I had to do wasn't quitting my job. It was creating space between myself and my parents—not because I wanted to, but because I needed to. I had to silence their voices just long enough to hear my own. I hope one day they understand that I didn't distance myself because I didn't love them. I did it because I do. Because I knew I could never truly give back to them if I didn't first choose myself.

Then came the real challenges—the days I questioned everything.

What am I doing?

Did I throw away stability for a dream that might not work?

Am I crazy?

What if I don't make it?

What if my parents were right?

But through all the doubt, one verse kept showing up in my heart: Walk by faith, not by sight.

For a whole year, I held onto that. When I spent hours editing a video only for it to flop. When I was scratching one idea for another, trying to figure out what I was even doing. When my bank account wasn't bank-accounting. When I felt unsupported. When doubt kept creeping in. I repeated it over and over again— *walk by faith, not by sight.*

Month by month, I kept showing up. I kept trusting. And slowly, I started to grow. I started to see little breakthroughs. I started to find my rhythm. And now, here I am—two years later, building a community, doing what I love, and most importantly, finally choosing me.

It wasn't one dramatic moment that changed everything, but a collection of little sparks that finally ignited my voice. A build-up of choices—choosing myself, choosing to speak, choosing to be seen. Each time I created something, I felt a little more free. I didn't realize it at the time, but by sharing my story, I wasn't just healing—I was making space for others to feel understood too. And slowly, I started speaking louder—not in volume, but in conviction.

Now, I find myself balancing two worlds. Nursing and content creation. By day, I'm caring for patients, administering medications, showing up in scrubs. By night—or rather, on the days I'm not nursing—I'm editing videos, writing captions, planning shoots, and pouring every ounce of my heart into this thing I'm building.

Sometimes, it really does feel like I'm living two lives.

There are days I wonder if I'm doing too much, or chasing something unrealistic. I've questioned whether people take me seriously. Whether I'm a nurse who happens to be creative—or a creator who still nurses. But every time I think about giving up, someone reaches out and says, "I needed this," or "You made me feel seen." And suddenly, all the tired nights and hard days feel worth it.

Because this isn't just about creating content; it's about *purpose.*

I'm still figuring it all out. Still navigating the balance between what I do to survive and what I do to thrive. But the difference now is—I'm walking in my purpose. I'm not ignoring that voice anymore. The one that kept whispering, *create, share, inspire.*

I may not have it all figured out, but I know this—

My story is only just beginning.

About the Author

Sarah Noelsaint is a Haitian-American content creator, and personal growth advocate, and multifaceted talent dedicated to helping others embrace confidence, self-worth, and intentional living. With a growing community of over 12.1K followers, she has cultivated an authentic space where she shares honest product reviews, self-improvement insights, and motivational content to empower others in their journey.

From a young age, Sarah was drawn to storytelling and creativity—whether through filming homemade videos, writing, or singing. While she initially pursued a career in healthcare, earning her LPN and RN designations, she realized her true purpose lay in content creation, beauty, and personal development. Now, as she transitions into a full-time creative career, she uses her platform to share her journey, inspire growth, and encourage others to step into their power.

Sarah blends beauty, wellness, and self-growth in her work—showing how self-care can be both an act of self-love and a tool for transformation. Through her work, she embodies confidence and individuality, encouraging others to embrace their authenticity and boldly pursue the life they dream of.

Recognized as a Top 40 Boston Influencer (Feedspot), Sarah has collaborated with major brands, including attending Huda Beauty's exclusive Blush Launch Event. But beyond accolades, what matters most to her is building a community that uplifts and empowers each other.

Through her content on TikTok, Instagram, and YouTube, Sarah shares beauty tips, self-care rituals, personal reflections, and vlogs that encourage resilience and growth. She strives to be a Proverbs 31 woman, embodying strength, faith, and purpose while guiding others toward their best selves.

https://sarahnoelsaint.com
Instagram: @sarahnoelsaint
TikTok: @sarahnoelsaint
YouTube handle: @sarahoelsaint

Dream in Focus

Lena Nugent

Part 1: A Small Town, A Big Dream

Growing up in Shumikha, a small Russian town of 30,000 people, I was always drawn to creativity. I played the piano, attended music school for seven years, and loved singing and dancing. I even had a band that performed in the city square during high school. During this time, my creative passion extended beyond music, and I started using my dad's camera to film clips for my classmates, capturing moments that made people feel something.

When it came time for university, I moved to Chelyabinsk, a much bigger city, to pursue higher education. I was a good student, balancing academic excellence with my artistic side. When I found a photography school, I knew I had to try. With nothing but a disposable camera, I captured an image of orange slices with a drop of juice and submitted it. My parents promised that if I got in, they would buy me a real camera.

That September, I was accepted, and in October, I was gifted my first professional camera: a Pentax K10D. That moment changed everything.

Alongside photography, I studied international relations, which led me to a life-changing opportunity in a work and travel abroad program. When I arrived in Boston, something inside me clicked. The energy, the opportunities... it felt like a place where I could truly belong. I knew I wanted to stay.

But falling in love with a place and building a life there are two different things.

Those first few months were overwhelming. I barely spoke English, and even though I had studied the language in school, real conversations felt impossible. But I adapted. I listened, I practiced, and I learned. Every interaction, every mistake, every awkward conversation pushed me forward. I forced myself to speak, even when I was embarrassed. Slowly, I found my rhythm. And with each passing day, Boston felt less like a foreign city and more like home.

While working at a café, I met a tall man with striking blue eyes. He came in every morning, ordering the same thing. Simple greetings turned into short conversations, then into something more. Eventually, we got married and had our daughter, Marina. My priorities shifted, and my life took a new direction.

Part 2: A New Life, A New Path

Marina was born the day before the Boston Marathon bombing. At Massachusetts General Hospital, where we were staying, the first two floors quickly filled up with victims. Having this happen in my new hometown was heartbreaking.

When we were finally discharged, the city was still on lockdown. Walking out of the hospital with my newborn in my arms, into a world filled with fear and uncertainty, felt like stepping into a different reality.

And yet, in the midst of that dark and cha

otic time, it was also the best day of my life—because I had her.

For three years, I was a stay-at-home mom, a role I cherished. Watching Marina grow, being there for every milestone... it was everything. But I had dreams beyond motherhood. I wanted more.

I earned my medical interpreter license and began working at Beth Israel Hospital, helping non-English-speaking patients communicate with doctors. It was fulfilling—I knew I was making a difference. That sense of purpose pushed me further. I didn't just want to facilitate communication; I wanted to treat patients myself. I shifted my studies to healthcare, working at major hospitals in Boston: Massachusetts General, Beth Israel, and St. Elizabeth's.

During this time, I went through a difficult divorce. I had to start over as a single mom. Photography lingered in my mind, but stability had to come first, so I threw myself back into my studies. One of my favorite memories from that time was doing chemistry homework with Marina on my lap. In the end, I graduated *summa cum laude* with a bachelor of science degree in exercise and health sciences. I was one step closer to becoming a physician assistant (PA).

Part 3: When the World Stopped, My Dream Began

But my love for photography never faded.

I met new people who reminded me how much I loved the art of photography. Still, the dream of having my own studio never left me. But as a single mom, I couldn't afford rent for both an apartment and a studio. So, I thought, why not create one in my living room? In February 2020, I transformed my tiny living room into a photography space. I bought cheap lights from

Amazon, the biggest backdrop they had, and set up my own studio in my three-meter-wide space.

Then, COVID happened.

With the world in lockdown, I had no clients, no shoots. But I had Marina.

On Marina's 7th birthday, we celebrated her in the middle of homeschooling and Zoom calls. She was my biggest cheerleader—and one of my very first models. I set up a pink backdrop, dressed her in a princess gown, and captured a moment of pure joy during an otherwise uncertain time. That was the moment I knew—I was meant to do this.

With all my free time, I researched studio photographers in Boston. I realized this city needed me. I had a fresh vision, something no one else had. I wasn't just another photographer; I was unique, and I was ready to prove it.

As restrictions lifted, I practiced on friends, experimented, learned. My first real model came in August 2020 for a free session. She posted the photos, and people noticed. My Instagram grew. My first paid session followed, and session by session, I built something real.

Part 4: The Hardest Choice: Security or Passion?

By May 2021, I was at a crossroads. I had everything I needed to apply to PA school, which was the safe, practical choice.

But my heart wanted something else.

I spent weeks wrestling with my decision, debating whether I should return to the medical field or fully commit to my growing photography business. I had built something out of nothing, a small, makeshift studio in my living room. My Instagram was growing, and clients were reaching out.

But would it be enough?

One night, I was having a conversation with a close friend about what I should do. Should I take the risk and pursue photography full-time? Or should I go back to school and follow the stable path I had spent so many years working toward? She looked at me, smiled, and said, "Just look at the back of your neck. The answer is there."

I reached up and remembered the tattoo I had gotten at 18: a small camera. I had chosen photography before I even knew I was choosing it.

I quit my hospital job.

I didn't apply to PA school.

I went all in.

And it was terrifying. But it was the best decision I ever made.

Part 5: From a Shared Space to My Own Empire

After three years of shooting in my home studio, I knew I had outgrown it. The space was too small for bigger teams or families, and I was ready to take the next step. I believe in manifestation, and just as that thought settled in, an opportunity presented itself.

I was invited to photograph an engagement party for celebrities from the UK, a session that ended up being published in *Hello!* magazine. At the event, I met another photographer, and we realized we had been following each other on Instagram but had never met in person. He mentioned his studio was looking for a sixth photographer, and I was intrigued.

When I visited the space, it was far from ideal: hot, messy, and uninspiring. But I saw potential. I loved the dark wood floors, the big windows, and the possibilities. For two weeks, I debated whether to look for a better space or take a leap of faith. The price was right, so I joined.

The studio wasn't ready for my clients, so I proposed a plan to improve it, but the other photographers weren't interested. No one wanted to invest in it.

So, I did it myself.

I spent thousands redesigning the space, making it beautiful, making it mine. As time passed, the other photographers left one by one, and eventually, the lease was transferred to my name. It was just me.

The first time I sat there alone in my studio, I cried. I had dreamed of this moment since photography school, and now, here I was, standing in a space that I built from the ground up, where my artistic visions could finally come to life.

Part 6: The Art of Seeing

Photography isn't just about taking pictures; it's about capturing energy, emotion, and movement. That's why people refer to me as "Not your average studio photographer." I don't believe in stiff, exaggerated poses. I focus on authenticity, letting my clients express themselves naturally, and in a way that feels true to who they are.

My style is cinematic, raw, and deeply personal. I don't chase perfection because perfection doesn't exist. Instead, I capture the in-between moments: the unfiltered laughter, the quiet confidence, the way someone truly exists when they forget the camera is there.

I work mostly with natural light, sculpting and highlighting features in a way that feels effortless. I guide my clients, helping them find their rhythm in front of the camera. One question I always ask is, "What's your favorite side?" Then, I shoot the other—to show them their beauty from all angles.

Society teaches us to see flaws; I see confidence, individuality, and light.

Over the last five years of working as a photographer, so many incredible people have shown me what my real purpose is. I'm not just here to take beautiful photos—I'm here to remind women of who they are, to show them their strength, and to help them build confidence. My purpose is to prove that every single person is beautiful. I deeply believe that every woman has her own unique light—and I'm here to help her see it.

When my clients tell me things like "I felt so comfortable with you," "I've never loved pictures of myself before," or "This experience meant so much to me," I know I'm doing exactly what I was meant to do. These aren't just sessions—they're moments of transformation. They're reminders that you are enough, you are beautiful, and you deserve to be seen.

When you step in front of my camera, you're not just being photographed—you're being seen.

This is why I do what I do. And why I will never be "just another photographer."

Part 7: Building a Dream—Motherhood and Entrepreneurship

People say, "If you work for yourself, you work twenty-four/seven." I never believed that... until I became a photographer.

Being a single mother and running a business is exhausting and rewarding. There are no fixed paychecks and no set hours—just the constant juggling of clients, emails, editing, and marketing. But amidst the chaos, I make time for what truly matters.

My daughter is my world. While I grow my business, I support her acting career—taking her to rehearsals, helping with auditions, and watching her shine on stage. We bond over our shared love for the arts, going to shows together, and chasing our creative dreams.

Beyond work and motherhood, I reset with volleyball in the summer, snowboarding in the winter, and yoga to stay grounded. I push myself to grow, taking photography courses to refine my craft.

But if there's one thing I've learned through it all, it's this: always trust yourself.

People told me photography wasn't a real career. That I needed something stable. That I should play it safe. But the thing about dreams is, they don't go away. They wait for you to be brave enough to chase them.

I came to this country as a first-generation immigrant, barely knowing the language, with no roadmap for my future. But I wasn't just here to exist—I was here to build something. To leave my mark.

I have two children—one is my daughter, the other is my business. They both require patience, resilience, and love. I've poured my heart into raising both, learning how to navigate motherhood and entrepreneurship at the same time, often without a safety net, often against the odds.

And I'm incredibly thankful to the people who believed in me and helped me along the way.

But I have never backed down.

Because this life I'm building isn't just for me—it's for Marina, for the future I want her to see as possible, for every person who needs proof that taking a risk on yourself is worth it.

Saying *yes* to myself despite the fear, the challenges, the unknown—this is what has shaped me.

Long after the shutter clicks and the session ends, the images remain. Proof of beauty, strength, and authenticity. A reminder of who we are.

I want to be an example for my daughter—to show her that dreams are worth chasing. That you don't have to choose between stability and passion—you can build both. That fear is not a stop sign; it's a challenge waiting to be conquered.

If you have a vision, believe in it.

If you have a passion, nurture it.

Because when you do, incredible things happen.

About the Author

Lena is a first-generation immigrant who came to the United States barely knowing the language and with no connections but with a relentless drive to build something extraordinary. Originally from a small town in Russia, she worked her way up, learning English, adapting to a new culture, and proving that resilience and passion can break any barrier.

Her journey has been anything but conventional. She spent years working in Boston's top hospitals as a medical interpreter, bridging the gap between patients and providers, before choosing to follow her true calling—photography. In 2020, she transformed her tiny living room into a home studio, turning uncertainty into an opportunity. Through hard work and vision, she built a thriving business, elevating her craft and creating a signature style that sets her apart.

But Lena isn't just a photographer—she's a strong role model for her daughter and a leader in her industry. She often says she has two children—her business and her daughter—both of which she nurtures with fierce dedication. She holds herself to the highest standard, constantly learning, growing, and pushing the limits of what's possible.

Beyond photography, she's an athlete and adventurer— snowboarding in the winter, playing volleyball in the summer, traveling to new countries and always striving for more. A true example of grit, grace, and ambition, Lena's story is proof that success is built, not given—and she's just getting started.

https://www.lenanugentphotography.com
https://www.instagram.com/lenanugentphotography

For More than Myself

Heather A. O'Connor, Esq.

"If you leave me, I will make sure that you have no money, no home, and that your kids will hate you. You will have nothing. In fact, you'll be lucky to even be able to sleep on a park bench at night." My ex-husband said this after I told him I wanted a divorce.

So, what did I do?

I stayed.

Why?

I was terrified that he had the power to actually carry through on his threats.

As much as I want to fast-forward and tell you about where I am now, it's important to first share where I came from with the hope that reading my journey will help you get through any tough time you might be facing or be able to overcome anyone telling you that you're not good enough or smart enough to achieve your goals.

I got pregnant just a few years out of high school, so I did what any girl who grew up in a religious household did: I got married. Although I ignored the other red flags, the first instance of physical abuse happened the night before my daughter's second birthday party when our second child was just six months old. I actually went to leave, but our elderly neighbor saw me crying while getting myself and the kids into the car and did what she thought was helpful. She reminded me that we are a really young family and that we needed to work through things because it was best for the kids. "He probably just had a bad day." Rather than leave, I just applied a lot of makeup to cover up the bruise on the side of my face so my daughter could have the birthday I had planned for her.

I did not get married to get divorced, but once you ignore abuse, it becomes easier to justify and ignore each time it happens again. You just have to figure out how to prevent a bad day; you learn to walk on eggshells. It did not help that we were significantly struggling financially.

After having our third child (because having more kids always makes life easier), my husband was arrested after he put his hands around my neck while my kids were home. An officer asked for permission to speak to my four-year-old son as he was skipping around the yard singing, "My Daddy got arrested!" The officer's words to me after changed my life: "Ma'am, we have to file a 51A with social services because when we asked your son if he understood why his Daddy had been arrested, he replied, 'Yes! Because he hurt my Momma like he hurts me.'"

That was my line in the sand, and I moved forward with filing for divorce.

What followed was a process that felt like I was on an emotional rollercoaster. Sometimes I'd be happy and excited about the possibility of a peaceful future. Other times, I'd feel scared, overwhelmed, lonely, sad, and a host of various other emotions that felt like they would come out of nowhere and just punch me in the gut.

And then came court. If you have never faced family court, for the most part, it's a horrible process when you're facing one of the lowest times of your life. You have a lawyer who says fancy words that you know can impact your future and your children's future but you do not truly understand what is going on. You know that if you are unable to come to agreements, a stranger dressed in a robe will hear about your entire life and make a quick judgment call on what happens to you within 15 minutes.

I sat in the hall waiting for my lawyer at the time to finish negotiating with my ex's lawyer when a woman sat down next to me:

"How is your lawyer?"

"I think good. It's hard to know."

"Yes, I feel the same way. Mine sounds good, but they don't really get it."

Her words lingered with me; she'd just made a very clear statement that expressed exactly how I felt. But what was the "it" that they weren't getting? As I lay in bed one night, it hit me: "It" was the empathy and understanding of what it's like to walk in a divorcee's shoes. "It" was understanding that emotional rollercoaster ride I desperately wanted to get off but knew I had to finish before I could exit. "It" was the bridge that needed to be built so a person could have a successful post-divorce life. The way I saw it, "it" was missing within most of what I witnessed during my many hours of sitting in court waiting for my mess of a case to be called. But what could I do about "it"?

One day my attorney said, "Heather, you are going to be financially responsible for raising three young kids, and you can't rely on the child support—have you come up with a plan on what you're going to do?"

And here comes my *Legally Blonde* moment:

"Oh yes! I'm going to go to college to become an attorney, and then I'm going to open a family law firm and change how divorce is done!"

My attorney started laughing until he realized I was dead serious. "That's a lot, Heather. Do you have any idea what you'd be getting into?"

"No. But I'll figure it out."

So, back to school I went, completely focused on achieving my goal. I started at Massasoit Community College in 2004, then attended U Mass Dartmouth, and finally graduated from Roger Williams University School of Law in 2011. I clerked for the chief justice of the Rhode Island Supreme Court for two years after law school, and then joined a boutique firm focused on family law.

In 2016, I finally opened O'Connor Family Law. Since then, we have grown into one of the most in-demand family law firms in Massachusetts, especially when it comes to high-conflict cases. We have grown into a team of over twenty people. We have been able to add a full-time client support coach to our team who provides complimentary coaching services to our clients while their case progresses with us. We have been able to help over one thousand families find closure and move forward to find peace.

I've been asked to share what has driven me to keep going through all the hard times—don't think for one moment I never doubted myself. I found those intrusive little thoughts creeping in constantly. Was I making the right choice? Was I putting myself before my kids? Would I actually be able to accomplish what I had started? I've also been asked what my proudest moment has been. The answer to both of these questions is the same.

While I was going through school, we moved to Fall River because I couldn't afford to live anywhere else. My daughter was in her first year of middle school and had been told she would be required to take Portuguese as a foreign language the following year. She informed the teacher that she didn't want to take Portuguese. She wanted to take Mandarin. In front of the whole class, the teacher told her that she had to take Portuguese because "You live in Fall River, and people don't leave Fall River. Everyone here speaks Portuguese, so you have to learn to speak Portuguese." My daughter rose from her seat and pointed to her fellow classmates, "Don't you tell me or anyone else in this room that we are stuck because of where we are. I watched my mom, and she came from nothing. But she is in law school, and she's going to become a lawyer. So if she can change her whole life, then you have no right to stand here and tell me and everyone else here that we are stuck because of where we come from."

As my daughter told me this story, I suddenly realized two things. First, my daughter was as fierce as they come, and I was so proud of her. Second, my journey was no longer just about me and my goals. My journey could be used to help show others that anything is possible. This made me more determined than ever, and anytime I felt discouraged or like giving up, I would think of all the other people who stood in my shoes, listening to their spouses tell them their lives would be over if they left. All the other people who felt stuck in life with little hope of things getting better. All the other people who'd been told they were not good enough or smart enough. For all of those people, I would reach my goals, and I would share both the ups and the downs along the way.

Today, I have accomplished more than I ever could have imagined as I stood in that courtroom hallway declaring that I'd be an attorney someday. And as wonderful as all of that is, it's nothing compared to hearing from people that they have gone on and accomplished things they were afraid of or not confident enough to do initially solely because they saw me do it first.

To me, that's what everything I do is all about.

About the Author

Heather O'Connor is a seasoned divorce attorney based in Boston, Mass., known for her compassionate approach and fierce advocacy in family law. As the founder of O'Connor Family Law, Heather has dedicated her career to guiding individuals through some of life's most challenging transitions with clarity, strength, and dignity. With over a decade of legal experience, she has earned a reputation not only for her strategic mindset in the courtroom but also for her ability to empower clients with knowledge and confidence.

Heather's own personal journey through divorce has shaped her empathetic, client-centered approach. She understands firsthand how overwhelming the legal process can be and works tirelessly to ensure her clients feel supported every step of the way. Her practice focuses on complex divorce cases, custody issues, and high-conflict situations, always with the goal of achieving the best outcome for her clients and their families.

Beyond the courtroom, Heather is a dynamic speaker and educator in the legal community, sharing insights on navigating divorce, co-parenting, and rebuilding life after separation. She's been featured in numerous legal publications and is recognized as a leader in transforming how divorce law is practiced in Massachusetts.

When she's not advocating for her clients, Heather is a devoted mom, entrepreneur, and community mentor. She believes in turning pain into power and uses her platform to help others reclaim their voice and future.

Heather O'Connor is more than a lawyer—she's a trusted ally during life's toughest moments.

Personal Facebook: @heatheroc92576

https://www.facebook.com/share/1EDaM3EwQZ/?mibextid=wwXIfr

Firm Facebook: @OconnorFamilyLawMA

https://www.facebook.com/share/18VJXGqhAv/?mibextid
=wwXIfr
Personal Instagram: @heatherocnr
Firm Instagram: @oconnorfamilylaw
www.familylawma.com

Collecting Beautiful Moments

Lexi Palumbo

How did you get into flowers?

"Well, I was selling cars."

"I'm sorry, huh?" *Cue the raised eyebrows and slight chuckle.*

"Yeah, I guess I should start from the beginning..."

It was the summer I graduated from college, a day I'll never forget. I was at my friend's house, lounging in the pool, when my phone rang. My father was on the other end, his voice urgent.

"Get down to the car dealership! Now!"

Apparently, he had been talking with his friend who owned a dealership, telling him, "Listen, this girl doesn't cook, she doesn't clean, and if I come home one more day at three p.m. and she's napping, I'm gonna lose my mind."

It was supposed to be a summer job until I found something more permanent. They started me in the back office doing social media work, but within a month, I noticed how much money the young guys on the sales floor were making. I thought to myself, *I could sell a car*. Three months later, I was the top salesperson, one of three women and a hundred men, and in four years I would become the youngest finance manager. I was building a career for myself.

And just like, another COVID story was born...

I went from sixty-five hours a week to forty. You'd think I would have embraced the extra time, maybe even enjoy having a bit of a social life again. But by that point, I had already become the ambitious and determined woman I am today. I needed more. The dealership's owner saw it too and made a suggestion that changed my life forever.

"You're always buying yourself flowers. Why don't you go work with our family florist?"

That's when I met my first mentor. I spent my half-days at the flower shop, learning how to properly process stems, how to cut a rose at just the right angle so it could drink more water, and how to properly green the foundation of your arrangement.

Working in that floral shop was transformative. For the first time, I was surrounded by a team of supportive women who lifted each other up. I had never experienced that before. And after that, there was no going back.

A few months later, one of my best friends called me with a new opportunity: "Would you be interested in doing a small event for my company? Just something simple for our clients at the park."

It was a small ask, but to me, it felt like the start of something big. On a whim, I filed for my LLC, thinking, *It's now or never*. I put together the event, filmed myself arranging flowers, designed custom cookies, and posted the video online.

It took just one post.

A friend from high school saw it and reached out, asking if I could do the flowers for her bridal shower.

The rest is history.

For as long as I can remember, my parents never missed an excuse to throw a party. They believed in celebrating every moment, no matter how small. So I believe that sense of joy and gathering had already been woven into the fabric of my DNA.

The past few years have been the wildest ride of my life. No one prepares you for exactly how hard "hard" is to start a business—if they did, no one would even step up to the starting line. But I'm beyond grateful I did.

That's why clichés like, "never easy, always worth it," exist; they're just true.

Life deserves to be celebrated. And I get to help people bridge the gap between the vision in their head and bringing it to life. I do more than just "throw a party" I create space for others to find reasons to come together. The world around us is changing so rapidly every day. I want my clients to enjoy their events worry-free, to be able to spend quality time with the people they love, and to show appreciation for them in ways they'll always remember.

As I step into this next chapter of my life, I hope you'll follow along. More than that, I hope this story inspires you. To take a chance on something different. To pivot from the path you thought was laid out for you. To understand that you don't need to have all the answers before you start.

You are capable of more than you know.

And if we connect, I hope one day, I'll be the one following your story, the one you were brave enough to write.

About the Author

Lexi Palumbo is the owner of Lexi Palumbo Floral Designs. Growing up, her family found every reason to celebrate, turning even the smallest moments into something special. That love for bringing people together naturally shaped her passion for floral design. She believes flowers are more than just décor; they set the tone, tell a story, and make memories unforgettable. Her goal is to help bring your vision to life and help you collect beautiful moments!

https://www.lexipalumbo.com

Instagram: @lexipalumbo

The Colorful Road to Healing and Joy

Katie Southworth

"So how long have you been painting?"

I always find this question tricky to answer. Sure, I always liked art growing up, but my dream was to be an Olympic gymnast, not an artist. There was, however, a moment I will never forget when painting transitioned from an intellectual curiosity to a profound healer.

I was working in the studio at Colby College during my senior fall semester. I had hit a creative block in the middle of a pink and orange painting. After what felt like hours of just staring at it, I started sobbing. Between cathartic tears, I realized that pink and orange are precisely my mother's aura colors: warm, energetic, loving, beautiful, and strong. Through the color, I could feel her love engulf me like a wave. It was grief, and it was the first time I felt a little lighter—one month after I lost her.

My mother, Ellie, was a tiny person—just over five feet and 120 pounds—but she had carried a heavy burden with incomprehensible strength for twenty-one years, since the moment I was born. She wanted my brother and me to grow up blissfully ignorant of her struggle with type II bipolar disorder. And we did.

Instead, we knew her as someone who lit up every room she entered. She was all our friends' "favorite mom" and could make any adult smile. When she asked you how you were, she actually meant it, and would actively listen. And then she would celebrate you with this fervor that often stopped people in their tracks. She just had this enduring light inside of her, and she uplifted everyone around her.

Unfortunately—and in keeping with the reality of type II bipolar disorder—what goes up, must come down. In the summer of 2015, Mom hit a low that completely extinguished her lightI had never seen her like that before. As strong a soldier as she was, over time, she had gotten tired. She won every battle over her lifelong struggle, but that summer the disease in her brain, armed with crippling intrusive thoughts, won the war. I got the call a week before my senior year, and in a second, every piece of me broke.

It's no coincidence that I discovered my signature style right after she died. In the same way that one can gain clarity on what's important in life after a major tragedy or loss, I found clarity on what was important to me in painting: color, light, and vertical line. I was intoxicated by the profound power of simplicity, by how much you can get from so little. Quite like how much joy you can get by doubling down on gratitude for your bare necessities. This is when the pink and orange painting happened—and then came twelve others just like it. By senior spring 2016, I had created a capstone series that won the Colby College Art Department's only merit-based award given each year. But more importantly, I had discovered a process that allowed me to emote, express, and share it all with others in a way that healed me more deeply than anything else.

I will carry scars on my shattered heart forever, but color put me back together... at least enough to carry on.

I know this now in hindsight—but at the time, I was twenty-two, about to graduate, and committed to pursuing a path in education. I had received degrees in psychology and studio art, but I was so hurt that I wanted to hide from anything that reminded me of my pain—painting included. That's when I moved to Boston instead of returning home to Connecticut or New York, where the loss of my mother was all too salient.

Here is what it sounds like to fit five post-grad years into one sentence: I completed a service year with Americorps (1); I got my master's degree from Tufts and paid for it by concurrently working an internship and three jobs (2); I immediately got hired by Boston Public Schools, and worked as an elementary art teacher for three years, half of which were during COVID-19 (3–5).

Yes, it felt exactly as crazy as it sounds. But it took me until after my first year of teaching was over to realize I was not OK. I was a shell of a human, putting no effort into life outside of work, nor any care into my mental or physical health. I took a hard look in the mirror and realized I had been trying to run from my grief in a frenetic, hyper-independent, all-out sprint. But life is a marathon, and grief is like a pet elephant: it's too heavy to drag along with you forever. You have to confront it, tame it, and let it go.

It became clear that if I wanted a shot at a balanced life, I needed to invest time into grieving, healing, and finding joy. I only had one idea of where to start: I decided I needed to paint again.

I can't make up this next bit—I consider it a moment of divine timing. I got the keys to my first studio in February 2020. I couldn't have known about the COVID-19 pandemic, the same way I was blindsided by my mom's death. And yet, during the most critical times of each crisis, I somehow set myself up to be painting.

That first studio was in the Sowa Artist Building on Harrison Avenue in Boston's South End. I spent every minute I wasn't teaching there, getting back in touch with my process. Thanks to the silver lining of COVID, there was an abundance of time to do so. The color coaxed the feelings out of me like animals that had burrowed for a long winter, sensing sunshine. Some of those feelings were joyful, exciting, and beautiful. Others were painful, ugly, and scary. But either way, every time, they were better out than in. Soon enough I felt brave enough to start sharing this thing that was healing me.

Because COVID had canceled all in-person opportunities, the only option for sharing my work was online... so I got to work; while many were learning how to make sourdough, I learned Instagram, website design, SEO optimization, video editing, email marketing, e-commerce, and social media networking.

The next thing I knew, I had made my first couple of sales and booked my first few commissions—that was the beginning of the snowball that is still rolling today. At that point, my main motivation to sell work was to be able to fund the studio itself, and buy more materials to make more work—frankly, that's still the main reason today! I simply wanted to fund my own method of self-care.

Eventually, I realized that each painting helped me learn something about myself; they were about sources of wellness and joy, moments of growth, processing love and loss, and how it all relates to being human and making life worth living. So I started writing about them. That's when my work went beyond healing me and started healing others.

Before I started writing I would hear feedback like:

It makes me so happy!

Wow, this is so calming.

It feels like a deep breath...

But after I started sharing my writing alongside the paintings, I started having *conversations*, where I started hearing things like:

Thank you for speaking honestly about that; no one does that.

I'm going through something right now, and this helped.

If I read that every morning it would change my life.

One woman even came to my studio to thank me personally. She said after learning my story she felt brave enough to sit her kids down and reveal that their grandmother—her mother—had lost her life to suicide, not natural causes. It was a family secret she had been keeping for fear of stigma her whole life, and she finally felt free.

That was one of the moments I realized I could be the change I wanted to see in the world. Another moment was when one of my students understood a lesson I had taught about living contemporary artists a little too well and asked:

"Wait, Ms. S, you're an artist too, right? And you're also our teacher? Why aren't you just an artist? That's like, so much cooler!"

In the summer of 2021, I realized I was back to being exhausted after accidentally morphing my healing hobby into more of a "jobby" on top of teaching. Something had to give or I risked losing my grip on my mental health again.

So I considered my options:

Do I keep building on my growing area of expertise, or accept the challenge of being a beginner again?

Do I add my own flare to a career many can do, or do I add my own career to the world, something only I can do?

Can I stand to spend my life asking "what if," or do I take a risk and live my life without regret?

Choosing the riskier life meant putting my joy, passion, and mental health first—and figuring out the rest along the way—in a world that typically asks you to do the opposite. It would demand investing in myself, betting on me, and believing in my art as the most unique and valuable thing I could offer the world. But the reward would be living a life bold and vibrant enough to honor my mom's legacy and make her proud.

In short, with my healing method as my north star, I was guided to who I was supposed to be, or who I had the power to be if I chose to. So, with the support of people who believed in me, I wrote my resignation letter in August 2021. Was I one hundred percent ready? Maybe not.

But like all gymnasts know, sometimes you just have to take that leap and trust your training to land it safely.

Today, I can proudly say that I have been supporting myself and giving back to mental health communities as a full-time artist ever since. I make all kinds of mistakes, and I am constantly learning, unlearning, trying, retrying, building, and rebuilding. My life and career are now very intertwined and constantly changing—no two days are the same, it is far from perfect, and I still miss my mom every day. But it is beautiful and I am in love with it because it is mine.

I have filled it with color because color makes me feel better, helps me process things, brings me clarity, and allows me to share my discoveries with you, in that order. The more I rinse and repeat that method, the closer I get to answers, manifestation, and hope for change.

When I feel lost, I come back to this: color is evidence of light, light is energy, energy is joyful, and joy is what makes us feel alive. Joy is the bridge between surviving and thriving. My job, as I see it, is to manipulate color in a way that harnesses the most possible joy, hope, and peace, for myself and others. I know a painting is done when it sings with a harmonious light that uplifts me the way my mom used to uplift others. It's elusive, but I know it when I see it. It is hard, but so is anything worthwhile.

Life will always be hard, but if we are bold, we get to choose our "hard." Grief, for example, is hard, but so too is mustering the bravery to choose joy anyway.

About the Author

Katie Southworth is an internationally collected, full-time, independent artist, author, and public speaker currently based in Bridgeport, Conn. Originally from Darien, Conn, she received bachelor's degrees in studio art and psychology from Colby College in 2016. She went on to receive her masters in teaching art from Tufts University in 2018 and taught visual art for Boston Public Schools for three years. Her fine art career started in the SoWa Design District of Boston in 2020, and she began pursuing art full-time in August 2021.

Katie moved her practice back to her home state of Connecticut in July 2023. Over 300 of her original works are in private and public collections across more than fifty cities in over half of the American states and abroad. She has shown in international art fairs such as Aqua Art Miami and has been featured in international, fine art, and local publications such as *Vogue, Create! Magazine,* and *Colby Magazine,* respectively. In April 2024 Katie published her first book, *Dr. Roy G. Biv: Healing One Colorful Painting at a Time, An Artist's Journey to Hope and Joy.* In honor of her mother Ellie, Katie donates a portion of her sales to the American Foundation for Suicide Prevention annually.

www.katiesouthworthart.com

@katiesouthworth_art

About the Curator, Leigh M. Clark

Four-time best-selling author Leigh M. Clark is known for her inspiring books, including *The Dream is in Your Hands*, *Living Kindly*, and the *Slay the USA* series. Her work as an author has empowered and motivated countless readers by highlighting kindness, resilience, and the strength of community. In addition to her writing career, Leigh has over 20 years of experience as a business strategist, working with Fortune 500 companies to help them grow and succeed.

Leigh's latest project, the Slay the USA series, is a growing national movement that shines a spotlight on extraordinary women across the country who are leaving their mark on their communities and industries. Through this series, Leigh is empowering these women to share their stories of triumph, leadership, and impact, much like she has done in her own life. The series is rapidly expanding, highlighting women in cities from coast to coast, celebrating their contributions and inspiring others to follow their lead.

Leigh's expertise and passion for leadership and empowerment have made her a sought-after speaker, with multiple appearances on the TEDx stage. Her stories of kindness and personal growth have been featured in prominent publications like *HuffPost* and shared through appearances on *The Today Show* and the *Rachael Ray Show.*

As the founder of Kindleigh, a movement focused on giving back through acts of kindness, Leigh has led initiatives that have raised significant funds for charitable causes. Her mission is to create lasting change through kindness and sharing stories of impact, further solidifying her role as a leader in philanthropy.

Leigh resides in Southwest Florida with her son, Carter, and the love of her life. She's here to make an impact and leave her mark by illuminating others.

"Don't let the world change your heart. Let your heart change the world." - Leigh M. Clark

Instagram:@leighmclark @slaytheusa

www.leighmclark.com

www.slaytheusa.com

www.ingramcontent.com/pod-product-compliance
Lightning Source LLC
Chambersburg PA
CBHW061750120626
46550CB00005B/1950